ChristWise

Discipleship Guide for Teens

Troy Fitzgerald

REVIEW AND HERALD® PUBLISHING ASSOCIATION
HAGERSTOWN, MD 21740

The author assumes full responsibility for the accuracy of all facts and quotations as cited in this book.

Unless otherwise indicated, all Bible texts are from the *Holy Bible, New International Version.* Copyright © 1973, 1978, 1984, International Bible Society. Used by permission of Zondervan Bible Publishers.

This book was
Edited by Gerald Wheeler
Copyedited by Delma Miller and James Cavil
Designed by Tina M. Ivany
Electronic makeup by Shirley M. Bolivar
Cover Photo by PhotoDisc
Typeset: Veljovic 12/16

PRINTED IN U.S.A.

06 05 04 03 02   5 4 3 2 1

R&H Cataloging Service
Fitzgerald, Troy, 1968-
    ChristWise

    1. Seventh-day Adventist—Doctrines   I. Title.

            268.433

ISBN 0-8280-1711-5

Other books by Troy Fitzgerald:
  ChristWise: Discipleship Guide for Juniors
  ChristWise: Discipleship Guide for Youth
  ChristWise: Leader's Guide for Juniors, Teens, and Youth

To order, call 1-800-765-6955.
  Visit us at www.reviewandherald.com for information on other Review and Herald® products.

If this book belongs to you, then it may be because you have made the decision to be baptized or are seriously thinking about it. Congratulations! There are several truths about baptism and preparing for baptism that are important to understand. Know first and foremost that while many people may be proud of you for taking this step, no one is more excited about your decision to follow Christ in baptism than the Father in heaven. Baptism represents the following wonderful things.

1. It signifies a desire to be born again (John 3:1-6; John 1:10-12).
2. It is a confession and asking for forgiveness of sins (Acts 2:38; Mark 1:5-9).
3. Through it the Father announces that we rightfully belong to Him (Mark 1:10-12).
4. It indicates death to the old self and the embrace of a new life (Romans 6:1-6).
5. We become part of a church family (1 Corinthians 12:13).
6. All heaven rejoices (Luke 15:7).

Repentance and baptism. Repentance simply means to "change your mind and turn your steps the other direction." People who want to be baptized usually have experienced a heartfelt desire to surrender their life to Christ and live fully for Him. As you continue to grow in God's grace it is my sincere hope that you will learn the great truths of Scripture and live in the certainty and joy of a relationship with the Savior.

***ChristWise* is** a journey through the teachings of the Seventh-day Adventist Church as portrayed in the life of Christ. It is our belief that Christ is the source and center of all of Scripture and that the doctrines describe the many ways

God's character and His love permeates this world of sin. The lessons rest on several building blocks.

1. Christ wants us to know Him personally, not just facts about the Bible. To know what day the Sabbath is or what happens to a person's body at death is only important as it emerges from the person of Jesus. Adventist faith involves a deep abiding knowledge and walk with Jesus.

2. Young people can actively study, experience, and live in ways that serve as examples to other believers. Since we learn best by doing, we have designed the lessons so that you can learn together with a partner as well as experience the Christian life individually.

3. Other people are important in the learning process. The *ChristWise* approach seeks to integrate young people with those who can serve not just as teachers, but as mentors—friends who join the journey of discipleship with you. The experiences and ideas of others in your congregation are significant tools for learning as well.

ChristWise **will** engage your heart and mind in a variety of ways:

Open Question: It includes questions that seek to get us thinking. Questions that prompt more than a yes or no from us. They encourage us to take a stand, to tell a story, and to make a choice. An open question fosters good thinking.

Opening Story: The lessons contain a short story or illustration that opens up the topic by getting to the heart of the issue. Such stories can make us laugh, cry, or even get mad. The opening story launches you into the study in which you can then approach the Word with a thoughtful mind.

Life of Christ: A section from Christ's teachings or a story from His life creates the perfect backdrop for the teachings of the Adventist faith. The lessons have as their goal discovering the many ways in which He tried to portray God's great plan for humanity.

We Believe: A statement of faith rooted in Scripture, it seeks to deepen your understanding and your knowledge of the Bible by encouraging you to mark up your Bible in a way that will help you to witness to someone else.

Way to Pray: Praying to God is like breathing. The lessons will prepare you to move beyond clichés to enable you to pray to God with power and sincerity. You will learn to pray about things that you never talked to God about before.

More Than Words: Take time to listen to people tell their stories. They will share their insights and ideas as you interview them with questions that will probe to the heart of the matter.

In the Mirror: Honestly looking inside our hearts and minds is a good way to grow up in Christ. Reflecting on how you have learned and what you think makes you morally and spiritually strong.

A few final tips before you start the journey:

Communicate clearly with your partner about the meeting time, expectations, and the things each of you need to bring.

Make this study a priority for you. Sometimes you may be tempted to sleep or watch TV instead of doing the work in this book. Commit yourself and your partner to remain faithful.

Don't breeze over any of the parts of this study. If you fall behind, save it for later. It is better to do just a little and do it thoughtfully than to rush through the whole study without letting it get into your heart and mind.

Be thinking about how you might become someone who is a leader/teacher or a mentor for someone else in the future.

The Scriptures

Opening Story

I stood at the back of the crowd, watching the magic show in the mall. Even more intriguing than the magician, however, was the girl beside me. She bawled like a burst pipe as the magician sliced a woman in half.

"It's OK, honey," her father said. "That woman didn't really get cut in half. It's just a trick. Let's go meet the magician, and he'll show you the woman is OK."

After the show the father escorted his girl to the stage. "Excuse me, sir, but your sawing trick greatly disturbed my daughter, Chelsea. Surely you will tell her that cutting a person in two is a trick, won't you?"

"Well—uh—of course the woman is OK and now in one piece . . ."

"But please show Chelsea that the woman is safe."

After 15 minutes of haggling, the magician surrendered his secret like a monkey giving up his last banana. "Of course she's OK. She is right there."

Because his assistant had changed out of her costume, however, the girl didn't recognize the woman. Ironically, even after the magician walked the girl through a step-by-step drill of the trick, the kid wouldn't buy it. Seeing the real thing did not equate to believing it.

Isn't it amazing how we can refuse to believe what is so clearly real? For example, science keeps documenting the deadly effects of tobacco, yet people still smoke. In a world swarming with sexually transmitted diseases young people remain as

promiscuous as ever. The Bible has been around for centuries and has proved itself to be the most trustworthy guideline for living. Nevertheless, many people ignore its counsel.

Why? Because we tend to believe the magic trick rather than the evidence. Consider the story Jesus told about the rich man and Lazarus.

Life of Christ

Luke 16:19-31

"There was a rich man who was dressed in purple and fine linen and lived in luxury every day. At his gate was laid a beggar named Lazarus, covered with sores and longing to eat what fell from the rich man's table. Even the dogs came and licked his sores. The time came when the beggar died and the angels carried him to Abraham's side. The rich man also died and was buried. In hell, where he was in torment, he looked up and saw Abraham far away, with Lazarus by his side. So he called to him, 'Father Abraham, have pity on me and send Lazarus to dip the tip of his finger in water and cool my tongue, because I am in agony in this fire.' But Abraham replied, 'Son, remember that in your lifetime you received your good things, while Lazarus received bad things, but now he is comforted here and you are in agony. And besides all this, between us and you a great chasm has been fixed, so that those who want to go from here to you cannot, nor can anyone cross over from there to us.' He answered, 'Then I beg you, father, send Lazarus to my father's house, for I have five brothers. Let him warn them, so that they will not also come to this place of torment.' Abraham replied, 'They have Moses and the Prophets; let them listen to them.' 'No, father Abraham,' he said, 'but if someone from the dead goes to them, they will repent.' He said to him, 'If they do not listen to Moses and the Prophets, they will not be convinced even if someone rises from the dead.'"

Open Questions

Do you think it is easier to believe your eyes or what was written years ago in the Bible? Why?

We Believe

The Holy Scriptures

Jesus spoke to the religious leaders so pointedly because they knew the Scriptures but didn't "live them." Read the statement below and mark or chain-reference the verses in your Bible.

"The Holy Scriptures . . . are the written Word of God, given by divine inspiration through holy men of God who spoke and wrote as they were moved by the Holy Spirit."* Everything we need for salvation is available in the Bible. The Bible is really about God revealing to us who He is and who we are in relation to Him. It reveals a trustworthy picture of God and becomes the authoritative guide for people as they follow Him.

a. 2 Peter 1:20, 21
b. 2 Timothy 3:16
c. Hebrews 1:1, 2
d. Hebrews 4:12
e. John 5:39
f. Psalm 119:105
g. Proverbs 30:5
h. 1 Thessalonians 2:13

i. James 1:22-25

Which verses help you understand the purpose of the Bible the most?

Write a brief statement of your belief about the Bible.

Way to Pray

Scan through Psalm 119 and notice what David says in prayer to God about Scripture. Write a short prayer to God about what you want to say to Him about His Word.

More Than Words

Interview someone you know about their faith in the Bible. Here are a few questions to ask them:

1. When in your life did you come to trust the Bible as God's word for you?
2. When has the Bible been a real source of strength to you? Have you had times when you had doubts about God's Word?
3. If you could tell only one story from Scripture, which one would you choose to help a friend know God? Why?

In the Mirror

Think about how important the Bible is to your life now. Does it point out some things in your life that you would you like to change?

* *Seventh-day Adventists Believe.*, p. 4.

The Trinity

Opening Story

Transworld Skateboarding asked some famous skateboarders the question, "Do you believe in God?" Here are some of the responses:

"Not in the traditional sense of a supreme being. I believe in a more unified force in the world."—Tony Hawk.

"I believe in my brain: God's in there, and it's really small. . . . We're just here, man. We don't know what's going on. All we know is that we don't know."—Tim O'Connor.

"I don't know if there is one physical man, but I do [believe in God] in one form or another."—Rick Howard.

"Yes, I do. I believe in God, and I think everyone has their own interpretation of what God is and who they know to be their God. I'm not really close with my god right now, but I do believe in God, for sure."—Reese Forbes.

"I believe there is something. I don't know if it's a someone, a female, or a male. I couldn't tell you what it is. But there's definitely something that is greater than ourselves. I do feel we were created somehow, but do I believe in God? I don't think I believe in God because God is just a word that was given to it. Like I could call my skateboard my god, you know?"—Ricky Oyola.

"No, I don't. I just can't see it. It's not real to me. It just feels like something so that people won't be so scared of dying—something to look forward to. I'm just meat and bones, and then it's done."—Rick McCrank.

"I do believe in something, you know? I don't know enough about God, you know? I know that I want to believe . . . I feel some spirit. Maybe if you just feel good about yourself and what you're doing . . . maybe that's what exists."—Brad Staba.

"Absolutely. I'm sure because something has to come from something. It can't just come from nothing. And we all know that there's a force that separates good from evil."—Rob Dyrdek.

"No. I don't believe in God. I think that when I die I'm gonna rot in the ground just like every other animal."—Moses Itkonen.

"Of course I believe in God. If you don't believe in God, then you think you're God."—Jamie Thomas.[1]

What do you think of their impression of God? A couple of thoughts popped into my mind as I thought about their answers:

The God I know not only wants us to know Him personally, but also goes out of His way to make it happen.

The God I know is a person, or has personlike qualities, for He created us "in His image."

The only way to really know God is through the ways He reveals Himself to us—primarily through Scripture.

As you study the Trinity, notice this supernatural encounter with Christ and think about what it really means both to believe in God and to know Him.

Life of Christ

Luke 24:36-49

"While they were still talking about this, Jesus himself stood among them and said to them, 'Peace be with you.' They were startled and frightened, thinking they saw a ghost. He said to them, 'Why are you troubled, and why do doubts rise in your minds? Look at my hands and my feet. It is I myself! Touch me and see; a ghost does not have flesh and bones, as you see I have.' When he had said this, he showed them his hands and feet. And while they still did not believe it because of joy and amazement, he asked them, 'Do you have anything here to eat?' They gave him a piece of broiled fish, and he took it and ate it in their presence. He said to them, 'This is what I told you while I was still with you: Everything must be fulfilled that is written about me in the Law of Moses, the Prophets and the Psalms.' Then he opened their minds so they could understand the Scriptures. He told them, 'This is what is written: The Christ will suffer and rise from the dead on the third day, and repentance and forgiveness of sins will be preached in his name to all nations, beginning at Jerusalem. You are witnesses of these things. I am going to send you what my Father has promised; but stay in the city until you have been clothed with power from on high.'"

Here is one of the many sections of Scripture that mention the Son, the Father, and the Holy Spirit in the same place.

What can you tell about the different roles that the members of the Trinity have by looking at this story?

We Believe

The Trinity

"There is one God: Father, Son, and Holy Spirit, a unity of co-eternal Persons. God is immortal, all-powerful, all-knowing, above all, and ever present. He is infinite and beyond human comprehension, yet known through His self-revelation. He is forever worthy of worship, adoration, and service by the whole creation." [2]

Trinity

    a. Deuteronomy 6:4
    b. Matthew 28:19, 20
    c. 2 Corinthians 13:14

The Father

"God the Eternal Father is the Creator, Source, Sustainer, and Sovereign of all creation. He is just and holy, merciful and gracious, slow to anger, and abounding in steadfast love and faithfulness. The qualities and powers exhibited in the Son and the Holy Spirit are also revelations of the Father."[3]

    a. Genesis 1:1

    b. John 3:16

    c. John 14:8-11

The Son

"God the Eternal Son became incarnate in Jesus Christ. Through Him all things were created, the character of God is revealed, the salvation of humanity is accomplished, and the world will is judged. Forever truly God, He became also truly man, Jesus the Christ. He was conceived of the Holy Spirit and born of the virgin Mary. He lived and experienced temptation as a human being, but perfectly exemplified the righteousness and love of God. By His miracles He manifested God's power and was attested as God's promised Messiah. He suffered and died voluntarily on the cross for our sins and in our place, was raised from the dead, and ascended to minister in the heavenly sanctuary in our behalf. He will come again in glory for the final deliverance of His people and the restoration of all things."[4]

    a. John 1:1-3, 14

    b. Luke 1:35

    c. Colossians 1:13-20

    d. John 10:30

The Holy Spirit

"God the eternal Spirit was active with the Father and the Son in Creation, incarnation, and redemption. He inspired the writers of Scripture. He filled Christ's life with power. He draws and convicts human beings; and those who respond He renews and transforms into the image of God. Sent by the Father and the Son to be always with His children, He extends spiritual gifts to the church, empowers it to bear witness to Christ, and in harmony with the Scriptures leads it into all truth."[5]

    a. Genesis 1:1, 2

    b. John 14:16-18, 26

    c. Acts 1:8

    d. Ephesians 4:11, 12

What do you believe about the Trinity—who God is—and what do you think is the best way to describe His many sides?

Way to Pray

As you pray this week, talk openly and honestly about what you think is true about God. Ask Him to reveal Himself to you in as many ways as possible. Prayerfully read through the Bible and discover what He might be trying to say about Himself.

More Than Words

Interview a teacher this week with the following questions:

When did you come to an understanding of the Trinity (God's threefold existence)?

How would you teach this to a fourth grader?

What do you know for sure about the Trinity, and what do you still have questions about?

In the Mirror

Write your thoughts on this mystery of God's existence. Share your own thoughts and questions as well with your partner.

---

[1] *Transworld Skateboarding,* p. 78.
[2] *Seventh-day Adventists Believe,* p. 16.
[3] *Ibid.,* p. 28.
[4] *Ibid.,* p. 36.
[5] *Ibid.,* p. 58.

The Great Controversy

Open Questions

Either/Or

"My beliefs determine my actions" or "My actions determine my beliefs." (Explain)

Can you think of examples of both mind-sets in the people you see today?

Opening Story

"Art Linkletter saw a small boy scrawling wildly on a sheet of paper. 'What are you drawing?' Linkletter asked.

"'I'm drawing a picture of God.'

"'You can't do that, because nobody knows what God looks like.'

"'They will when I'm finished,' the boy confidently replied."[1]

A. W. Tozer once said that the most important thing about us is what we believe about God. Perceptions—the way we see things—are powerful. The perception I had of my next-door neighbor scared me to death. Mr. Rob was tall and bony with a bushy gray mustache and an Adam's apple the size of—well, an apple. Because he just looked weird, he made me nervous.

One night as we were eating at the dinner table Mr. Rob did something to alter my view of him entirely. I watched him nervously because I never knew when he would attack. During the middle of the meal his expression changed from scary to downright silly. I giggled at the sight. His face returned to its normal scary pose for a moment, then he repeated his silly look when no one else was watching. By now my eyes were riveted on him as I took another bite.

Like the final explosion of fireworks on the Fourth of July Mr. Rob rapidly contorted his face, repeating in a sensational show of tremendous talent all the expressions he had made during dinner. The food in my mouth spewed out like a volcano as I laughed uncontrollably. I laughed so hard that my dinner made its way through my nose, ears, and I think through my eyelids. My mother and father stared in horror at me as Mr. Rob's face effortlessly resumed its gaze back at his plate of food. While I was scolded for my bad manners, I changed my mind about my skinny neighbor. He wasn't a freak—he was a riot. Mr. Rob became an endearing part of my family, and during the years following I saw what the rest of my family had already observed—a brilliant, witty, caring human whose passion in life was to create a moment of artistic surprise.

Perceptions. The fight between Christ and Satan is about perceptions and beliefs. Lucifer—tainted by pride and self-exaltation—saw God as a tyrant. As a result, he deceived the angels and now seeks to convince the world to believe a lie about God's character. The bottom line? The target of Satan's fiery darts is our mind—what we think of God and what we believe God thinks of us. If Satan can reshape our perspective—our viewpoint—only a little, it is enough to taint, even destroy, our relationship with our Father in heaven. Notice the battle in the life of Jesus.

Life of Christ

Luke 11:14-20

"Jesus was driving out a demon that was mute. When the demon left, the man who had been mute spoke, and the crowd was amazed. But some of them said, 'By Beelzebub, the prince of demons, he is driving out demons.' Others tested him by asking for a sign from heaven. Jesus knew their thoughts and said to them: 'Any kingdom divided against itself will be ruined, and a house divided against itself will fall. If Satan is divided against himself, how can his kingdom stand? I say this because you claim that I drive out demons by Beelzebub. Now if I drive out demons by Beelzebub, by whom do your followers drive them out? So then, they will be your judges. But if I drive out demons by the finger of God, then the kingdom of God has come to you.'"

We Believe

The Great Controversy

"All humanity is now involved in a great controversy between Christ and Satan regarding the character of God, His law, and His sovereignty over the universe. This conflict originated in heaven when a created being, endowed with the freedom of choice, in self-exaltation became Satan, God's adversary, and led into rebellion a portion of the angels. He introduced the spirit of rebellion into this world when he led Adam and Eve into sin. This human sin resulted in the distortion of the image of God in humanity, the disordering of the created world, and its eventual devastation at the time of the worldwide flood. Observed by the whole creation, this world became the arena of the universal conflict, out of which the God of love will ultimately be vindicated. To assist His people in this controversy, Christ sends the Holy Spirit and the loyal angels to guide, protect, and sustain them in the way of salvation."[2]

a. Revelation 12:4-9

b. Isaiah 14:12-14

c. Ezekiel 28:12-18

d. Genesis 3

e. Genesis 6-8

f. 2 Peter 3:6

g. 1 Corinthians 4:9

Which verse speaks to you the most about this topic? Why?

What do you believe about the war between Christ and Satan? In a few sentences, describe how you would teach this to a third grader.

Way to Pray

Take a few moments and write down all the characteristics you can think of about God. In your prayer life this week talk to Him about the character traits you love and are grateful for, and also those qualities you don't quite understand.

More Than Words

Interview a college student this week and ask them the following questions:

How has your view of God changed in the past 10 years?

When in your life have you been most aware that the battle between good and evil involves you personally? Describe that time or the events surrounding it.

What advice would you give a teenager who is seeking to know who God "really" is in a world that misunderstands or misrepresents Him?

In the Mirror

Think about the war between Christ and Satan. What do you believe it was like back when it started? How do you think it will end?

---

[1] Erwin Lutzer, *Ten Lies About God,* p. 1.
[2] *Seventh-day Adventists Believe,* p. 98.

The Experience of Salvation

LESSON 4

Open Questions

Rank the stories in order of their powerful message of salvation to the lost—1 being the most powerful and 5 being the least powerful to you:

___ The story of the woman caught in adultery and saved from stoning

___ The story of Zacchaeus and his conversion and renewed lifestyle

___ The leper who came to Christ for healing

___ The story of the thief on the cross who received eternal life through faith

___ The woman who touched the hem of Jesus' garment and was healed of her sickness

Why did you rank them in this order?

Opening Story

As I looked out the window of the bus everything was a blur. No, my eyes were not filled with tears and I was not taking hallucinogens. Nor was I suffering from depression and confusion. It was a time when the "wet look" was in, and I always managed to sit in a seat on the bus that had the view of the window distorted by gooey, slimy hair gel (I hope it was hair gel). My two-hour bus ride every day always made me sleepy, but I fought the sleep for fear my head would lean against the window smeared with the yuck. On this particular day, though, I fell fast asleep. Fortunately, my head rolled backward, protecting my hair.

I awoke to the voice of the bus driver announcing, "Last stop!" As I leaped from my seat I felt a cold chill creep over my heart when I saw that the bus was empty, save for the driver and me. "You gotta get off here, pal," the man said. I tried to find a clear piece of window to get my bearings, but couldn't recognize a thing.

"Where are we?"

The bus driver looked at me in disbelief. "You missed your stop, didn't you?" I got off the bus into unknown territory and wanted to cry. It was 5:00 p.m., and my parents would be stuck in traffic and wouldn't be home for a while. I was stranded. Lost. Alone.

Then the sound of a honking car jerked me from my misery as a friend from school pulled up to the bus stop. Christina leaned out the window, shouting, louder than she needed to, "Did you forget to get off at your stop?" It was more of a statement than a question (she always seemed to enjoy humiliating me in public). Glad to see Christina and her mom, however, I didn't care how loud she shouted. She and I took the same bus route, so when she got off and I didn't, she suspected I had been asleep or not paying attention. "When I didn't see you get off the bus," she explained, "we decided to come after you. Finally we caught up with you."

"Actually I thought I'd do a little shopping down here," I felt tempted to tell her. Instead I jumped into her car and confessed, "I fell asleep and woke up way too late." They both looked at my hair, knowing how dangerous sleeping on buses could be. "I can't tell you how glad I am to see you." I rode the rest of the way home with my heart in my throat and a hint of a smile on my face—it was good to be "not lost."

Being lost and being found are two tremendously different experiences, and what happens in between is an incredible journey. The parable of the prodigal son is, I believe, *the* story of the experience of salvation. As you read it, underline or highlight the parts that you think are key words or phrases because they say something about how we are saved and from what are we saved.

Life of Christ

Luke 15:10-24

" 'In the same way, I tell you, there is rejoicing in the presence of the angels of God over one sinner who repents.' Jesus continued: 'There was a man who had two sons. The younger one said to his father, "Father, give me my share of the estate." So he divided his property between them. Not long after that, the younger son got together all he had, set off for a distant country and there squandered his wealth in wild living. After he had spent everything, there was a severe famine in that whole country, and he began to be in need. So he went and hired himself out to a citizen of that country, who sent him to his fields to feed pigs. He longed to fill his stomach with the pods that the pigs were eating, but no one gave him anything. When he came to his senses, he said, "How many of my father's hired men have food to spare, and here I am starving to death! I will set out and go back to my father and say to him: Father, I have sinned against heaven and against you. I am no longer worthy to be called your son; make me like one of your hired men." So he got up and went to his father. But while he was still a long way off, his father saw him and was filled with compassion for him; he ran to his son, threw his arms around him and kissed him. The son said to him, "Father, I have sinned against heaven and against you. I am no longer worthy to be called your son." But the father said to his servants, "Quick! Bring the best robe and put it on him. Put a ring on his finger and sandals on his feet. Bring the fattened calf and kill it. Let's have a feast and celebrate. For this son of mine was dead and is alive again; he was lost and is found." So they began to celebrate.' "

We Believe

The Experience of Salvation

"In infinite love and mercy God made Christ, who knew no sin, to be sin for us, so that in Him we might be made the righteousness of God. Led by the Holy Spirit we sense our need, acknowledge our sinfulness, repent of our transgressions, and exercise faith in Jesus as Lord and Christ, as Substitute and Example. This faith, which receives salvation, comes through the divine power of the Word and is the gift of God's grace. Through Christ we are justified, adopted as God's sons and daughters, and delivered from the lordship of sin. Through the Spirit we are born again and sanctified; the Spirit renews our minds, writes God's law of love in our hearts, and we are given the power to live a holy life. Abiding in Him we become partakers of the divine nature and have the assurance of salvation now and in the judgment."*

a. John 3:16

b. Romans 3:21

c. 2 Corinthians 5:17-21

d. Galatians 4:4-7

e. Titus 3:3-7

f. Romans 8:14-17

g. Romans 10:17

h. Galatians 3:2

i. Romans 8:1-4

j. Romans 12:2

Which three verses especially speak to you about the experience of salvation? Why?

How would you respond to someone asking you, "So, how can I know that I am going to go to heaven?"

Way to Pray

As you have looked at what it means to experience salvation, offer with your partner a prayer that recognizes that you are lost, that you believe in the free gift of grace, and that you accept the assurance of salvation with joy and confidence. Continue to pray throughout the week a prayer of thanksgiving for the work God has done for you on Calvary.

More Than Words

After Jesus had healed the man possessed by demons He him, "Go home to your family and tell them how much the Lord has done for you, and how he has had mercy on you" (Mark 5:19).

Write a letter to someone who has had a big influence on your life. Tell them about your decision to receive Christ into your life and thank them for their support, then mail it to them or even deliver it personally. (Share in a few words how writing the letter affected you.)

Interview someone who you believe has made a heartfelt decision to follow Christ, using the following questions:

When did you first admit your need of a Savior and invite Christ into your heart? What were the circumstances and how did it happen?

Have you ever doubted the fact that you were saved? If so, how do you respond to such doubts?

What Bible passage best describes the salvation experience to you?

In the Mirror

As you think about your decision to follow Christ, what excites you and what makes you a little nervous? How do you think you should respond to such feelings?

* *Seventh-day Adventists Believe*, p. 118.

Baptism

Open Questions

When do you think a person is ready for baptism? Why?

What is the most memorable baptism you have ever witnessed? Why?

Opening Story

A parable: A teenage girl (we'll call her Susan) once became so filled with anger against her parents she decided to run away from home. She scribbled her hatred toward them on a note she left on the breakfast table. "This is my certificate of divorce," she said. "You are no longer my parents. I am no longer your daughter. I'm gone. This divorce is final." And she left just before dawn.

Now, normally when young people run away they go around the block, get hungry, forget their anger, and return home. Not Susan. She was long gone by the time her parents awoke and found the note. The girl hitchhiked her way across the state and into another part of the country. Finally she felt free. Meanwhile, her parents searched frantically for her. The police, the sheriff's office, and the FBI all were looking for Susan, but could not find her anywhere. For three and a half years the parents continued the search, hoping they would find their daughter.

One morning the phone rang and a deep voice on the line said, "We think we have found your daughter. She is alive but part of a prostitution and drug ring, and since she is 17 now, we can't force her to return home to you. We can ask her, and if she responds positively, we will get her out of there and bring her to you. Would you like to send her a message?"

"Yes, tell her we love her and for her to please come home," the mother replied.

The authorities approached the young woman, who was too young to be living on the streets and in seedy hotel rooms. When the message from her parents reached her ears, the empty life she now lived could not match her memories of the safety and comfort she had once known. She returned with the agents to her home.

Needless to say, her mother and father welcomed her with joy. Her room was unchanged. The pictures remained on the walls. For several weeks she tried to settle into the home of her childhood, but something was wrong. The relationship was awkward. Although her mom and dad never once mentioned the way she had left, she remembered clearly the words she wrote and the agony she had put her parents through.

One morning she came downstairs and placed a piece of paper on the table before her parents. On the top of the page were the words "Certificate of Adoption." She drew up an agreement for adoption with a place for her and her parents to sign. Her signature was already on the bottom of the page. Confused, her father looked at her. "Susan," he said cautiously, "I can't sign this. You are my daughter. We have always been your parents. We didn't sign your divorce papers, and we won't sign this. You belong to us, as you have always."

As Susan put her arms around her mom, tears welled up in her eyes. "I know how you feel about me. This is not for your benefit, but for mine. I chose to leave, and this is my way of choosing you back. I need to say this. Please, please do this for me and let me choose you formally." Her parents understood, and both signed the agreement. A smile crept across Susan's face as she signed under the line entitled "Daughter."

From God's point of view you have always been His child. Because of our fallen condition, we must die to our old self and be "born again." The word for it is baptism, a public and formal statement of your decision to be in His family—to be His child. Baptism is like Susan's declaration of adoption. But believe me, when it happens, all heaven erupts with shouts of praise as we formally call God "Father."

Notice how the people came in the days of Christ to signify their surrender to God and claim Him as their Father. As you have made this choice, consider the words spoken at the baptism of Jesus, and recognize that the Father declares them at yours.

Life of Christ

Mark 1:2-11

"It is written in Isaiah the prophet: 'I will send my messenger ahead of you, who will prepare your way'—'a voice of one calling in the desert, "Prepare the way for the Lord, make straight paths for him."' And so John came, baptizing in the desert region and preaching a baptism of repentance for the forgiveness of sins. The whole Judean countryside and all the people of Jerusalem went out to him. Confessing their sins, they were baptized by him in the Jordan River. John wore clothing made of camel's hair, with a leather belt around his waist, and he ate locusts and wild honey. And this was his message: 'After me will come one more powerful than I, the thongs of whose sandals I am not worthy to stoop down and untie. I baptize you with water, but he will baptize you with the Holy Spirit.' At that time Jesus came from Nazareth in Galilee and was baptized by John in the Jordan. As Jesus was coming up out of the water, he saw heaven being torn open and the Spirit descending on him like a dove. And a voice came from heaven: 'You are my Son, whom I love; with you I am well pleased.'"

We Believe

Baptism

"By baptism we confess our faith in the death and resurrection of Jesus Christ, and testify of our death to sin and of our purpose to walk in newness of life. Thus we acknowledge Christ as Lord and Saviour, become His people, and are received as members by His church. Baptism is a symbol of our union with Christ, the forgiveness of our sins, and our reception of the Holy Spirit. It is by immersion in water and is contingent on an affirmation of faith in Jesus and evidence of repentance of sin. It follows instruction in the Holy Scriptures and acceptance of their teachings."*

    a. Romans 6:1-6
    b. Acts 2:38
    c. Acts 16:30-33
    d. Acts 22:16
    e. Colossians 2:12, 13
    f. Matthew 28:19, 20
    g. 1 Corinthians 12:13

As you study the passages that deal with baptism, which one speaks to you the most about your decision to be baptized? Why?

Way to Pray

As you pray this week, think about the words of Paul, who said, "I have been crucified with Christ and I no longer live, but Christ lives in me. The life I live in the body, I live by faith in the Son of God, who loved me and gave himself for me" (Galatians 2:20).

More Than Words

Make the plans for your baptism, selecting the date, place, pastor, songs, text, testimonies, etc. Then, as you prepare for it, interview an older friend in the church about baptism and ask them the following questions:

What was the most memorable part of your baptism?

What is the significance of baptism as you see it?

If you could again prepare for baptism and plan for the event, what would you do differently?

In the Mirror

Think about your own decision to follow Christ in baptism. What events, people, and experiences have brought you to this decision?

---

* *Seventh-day Adventists Believe*, p. 180.

Creation

Open Questions

Share a time in your life when you thought you were absolutely right and turned out to be dead wrong. What was it like?

Opening Story

"An 8-year-old waving around a $100 bill? He says he earned it? Yeah. Right! He stole the $100 bill, because 8-year-olds don't earn money."

"A corn farmer running for mayor? Only educated people are smart enough for politics. There's no way I'd vote for him, because farmers don't have to make big decisions."

"If you should happen to contract a disease, fever, or inflammation, the best remedy is to either apply leeches or simply poke a hole in the infected area or the region of the pain and let the blood out. Since the ailment travels through the bloodstream, just get rid of the bad blood."

What do you see in these statements? They are ridiculous, full of prejudice, ignorance, and illogic. Although wrongheaded, they are real and stubbornly defended.

Once I asked my 4-year-old son, "Do you want to golf with me and Uncle Mike this weekend?" He responded without missing a beat, "Dad, I can't because I don't even have a fishing pole."

At first I scratched my head, then it dawned on me that while on vacation we had stayed at a hotel in which the artwork in the lobby had golf pictures next to fishing pictures. Somehow he just connected the two together. You can't really have one without the other, can you? The point is this: Many popular ideas get born out of bad logic or some wild notion that popped into someone's thoughts.

In 1990 the 8-year-old mentioned above won a poetry contest entitled "My Shoes Are Too Tight," in which the grand prize was a $100 bill. The Midwest farmer became mayor, winning by a landslide. Why? He was brilliant, and almost everyone in the town was familiar with his innovative spirit and decision-making skills. He had a degree in biology, but even if he didn't, the fact remains that I have never met a farmer who wasn't sharp as a razor. At one time bloodletting seemed to be a logical remedy for disease. If someone is sick now, would we drain off their blood?

How could people think in such ways? As in the story of the blind man healed by Christ, the critics miss the truth because they already believe something else. See if you can see in the following story some patterns of thinking that people today still have. At the end of the story notice the last two sentences and discuss them with your partner.

Life of Christ

John 9:1-16

"As he went along, he saw a man blind from birth. His disciples asked him, 'Rabbi, who sinned, this man or his parents, that he was born blind?' 'Neither this man nor his parents sinned,' said Jesus, 'but this happened so that the work of God might be displayed in his life. As long as it is day, we must do the work of him who sent me. Night is coming, when no one can work. While I am in the world, I am the light of the world.' Having said this, he spit on the ground, made some mud with the saliva, and put it on the man's eyes. 'Go,' he told him, 'wash in the Pool of Siloam' (this word means Sent).

So the man went and washed, and came home seeing. His neighbors and those who had formerly seen him begging asked, 'Isn't this the same man who used to sit and beg?' Some claimed that he was. Others said, 'No, he only looks like him.' But he himself insisted, 'I am the man.' 'How then were your eyes opened?' they demanded. He replied, 'The man they call Jesus made some mud and put it on my eyes. He told me to go to Siloam and wash. So I went and washed, and then I could see.' 'Where is this man?' they asked him. 'I don't know,' he said. They brought to the Pharisees the man who had been blind. Now the day on which Jesus had made the mud and opened the man's eyes was a Sabbath. Therefore the Pharisees also asked him how he had received his sight. 'He put mud on my eyes,' the man replied, 'and I washed, and now I see.' Some of the Pharisees said, 'This man is not from God, for he does not keep the Sabbath.' But others asked, 'How can a sinner do such miraculous signs?' So they were divided."

We Believe

Creation

"God is Creator of all things, and has revealed in Scripture the authentic account of His creative activity. In six days the Lord made 'the heaven and the earth' and all living things upon the earth, and rested on the seventh day of that first week. Thus He established the Sabbath as a perpetual memorial of His completed creative work. The first man and woman were made in the image of God as the crowning work of Creation, given dominion over the world, and charged with responsibility to care for it. When the world was finished it was 'very good,' declaring the glory of God."*

    a. Genesis 1
    b. Genesis 2
    c. Exodus 20:8-11
    d. Psalm 19:1-6
    e. Psalm 33:6, 9

f. Psalm 104

g. Hebrews 11:3

Which verse speaks to you the most about this topic?

Write a statement that describes what you believe to be true about God's work of creation.

Way to Pray

In Job 38 to 40:6 God reminds Job and us who He is. God asks a series of questions about the created world, questions that only a Creator could answer. Breeze through them and look at Job's response in Job 40:4, 5. As you pray this week, pray to God as a close Friend and a mighty Creator.

More Than Words

Interview: Invite someone to share their thoughts on the following questions:

When have you been most awed by God's creative work? Describe what you experienced and why you think it was so powerful.

What story or passage from Scripture stands out as a compelling piece of evidence for God's creative power?

Why do you think people so widely accept evolution in today's world?

In the Mirror

What do you think are the most effective ways for you personally to stay in touch with God as a Creator?

* _Seventh-day Adventists Believe,_ p. 68.

The Law of God

During my first year in college, before I learned to cook, I learned to heat. The culinary skill of heating is by far the most important tool of the bachelor who gets hungry. Today people look down upon the archaic methods of boiling, baking, and "slowly simmering" anything. Heating by microwave is the only way to go. The food that presents the greatest challenge, though, is the frozen burrito.

I returned from my classes starving for something cheap, filling, and easy to prepare. My heart sank into my vacant stomach as I opened the door to my refrigerator. Seeing nothing that resembled a meal, I ventured into the freezer. There they were—frozen burritos. *Oh, great, frozen burritos!* I thought. *Now I have to slave over a hot microwave (at least I think it is hot in there) for at least two minutes before I can eat.* It seemed like a year before the three beeps announced the end of the wait. I grabbed the burritos, carefully left in their plastic package with the ends partially open (a technique popular among young bachelors during the eighties).

Unfortunately, the burrito was so hot that I had to drop it on a small, uncluttered landing space on the counter reserved for just such emergencies. Using a few utensils, a paper plate, and a ravenous appetite, I lunged into the burrito with my fork. The fork cut smoothly into the tortilla, then stopped cold about halfway through the burrito. "No!" It was still frozen. The heat had never penetrated deep enough to heat the inside. The choice? Heat it or eat it. But what does this have to do with God's law?

One time Jesus declared, "Unless your righteousness [rightdoing] surpasses that of the Pharisees and the teachers of the Law, you will not enter the kingdom of heaven." Such news would sap His listeners of their hope for eternal life. Why? All knew the unparalleled obedience of the Pharisees. To imagine anyone being even better was unimaginable. But Jesus makes it clear that the way the Pharisees obeyed the law was a lot like heating the frozen burrito: The heat has to go into the heart of the burrito for it to be good. John referred to it this way: "This is love for God: to obey his commands. And his commands are not burdensome, for everyone born of God overcomes the world. This is the victory that has overcome the world, even our faith" (1 John 5:3, 4). The love and power of God's revealed will in His law must be a matter of the heart—and not just the skin—for it to be meaningful.

Life of Christ

Matthew 5:17-20

"Do not think that I have come to abolish the Law or the Prophets; I have not come to abolish them but to fulfill them. I tell you the truth, until heaven and earth disappear, not the smallest letter, not the least stroke of a pen, will by any means disappear from the Law until everything is accomplished. Anyone who breaks one of the least of these commandments and teaches others to do the same will be called least in the kingdom of heaven, but whoever practices and teaches these commands will be called great in the kingdom of heaven. For I tell you that unless your righteousness surpasses that of the Pharisees and the teachers of the law, you will certainly not enter the kingdom of heaven."

We Believe

The Law of God

"The great principles of God's law are embodied in the Ten Commandments and exemplified in the life of Christ. They express God's love, will, and purposes concerning human conduct and relationships and are binding upon all people in every age. These precepts are the basis of God's covenant with His people and the standard in God's judgment. Through the agency of the Holy Spirit they point out sin and awaken a sense of need for a Saviour. Salvation is all of grace and not of works, but its fruitage is obedience to the Commandments. This obedience develops Christian character and results in a sense of well-being. It is an evidence of our love for the Lord and our concern for our fellow men. The obedience of faith demonstrates the power of Christ to transform lives, and therefore strengthens Christian witness."*

a. Exodus 20:1-17

b. Psalm 40:7, 8

c. Matthew 22:36-40

d. Deuteronomy 28:1-14

e. Matthew 5:17-20

f. John 15:7-10

g. 1 John 5:3

h. Psalm 19:7-14

What verse speaks to you the most about this topic?

As a Christian, how do you explain the importance of the law and also the reality that we are saved by grace, not by our efforts?

Way to Pray

As you pray this week, consider areas of God's law that you struggle with obeying consistently. Talk specifically to God about those problems and invite Him to remind you about them and to strengthen you to be faithful.

More Than Words

Ask the following questions of a young adult you admire and respect:

How did you relate to rules as a teenager?

When did you personally come to understand the value of God's law in your own life?

How does a person get God's law written on their heart? What does that look like to you in everyday life?

In the Mirror

Think and write about the commandments you want written on your heart the most at this stage of your life.

---

* *Seventh-day Adventists Believe*, p. 232.

The Sabbath

Open Questions

When have you been so frustrated that you were a little out of control? What happened?

Opening Story

The graffiti on the side of the church left me more than frustrated—I was downright mad. The local boys thought their artwork was more pleasing to the eye than our plain white paint on the masonry block walls of the church. I knew the kids who did it but could never catch them in the act. Then I remembered something in my younger days as an assistant boys dean. The head dean and I were painting the halls of the dorm and the paint wouldn't stick—it simply peeled off. "What is up with this paint?" we wondered aloud. The guy at the paint store gave us the answer: epoxy paint. The only thing that will stick to epoxy paint is epoxy paint. Amazing stuff, it is one part paint and one part glue. The stuff will not come off.

When I remembered my previous experience with the substance, the deacons and I painted the side of the church with a serious coat of epoxy paint and waited.

After a week or so, I parked my car on the other side of the street and watched for the vandals to do their sinful work. They never came. So I went looking for them in the neighborhood. I found them all hanging out on someone's front yard looking bored and mischievous. Jumping out of the car, I yelled, "You guys got to come to the church and see what someone did to the walls!" Then I muttered a prayer for them to follow me on their bikes and skateboards back to the church. I waited there by myself, staring at the bright white walls. They snickered as they rode up. (Suckers.)

"Do you see this wall?" I announced proudly. "Doesn't it look great?" Their grins broadened as they looked at each other like a bunch of vultures perched over a dying animal. They must have thought that I had lost my mind or was a complete idiot. I had them.

"Yeah, man. That's a really nice paint job," they all chuckled.

"Thanks," I replied proudly. "I did it myself."

"Hope nobody tries to mess it up, man," the ringleader mentioned with a total lack of sincerity.

The others snickered. "Yeah, that would be a real tragedy, dude, someone coming and messin' it all up," another added.

I put on my most shocked look. "You really think someone might try that?" I said with a genuine note of concern.

They smirked. "I don't know. It is a rough neighborhood and all," the ringleader said.

At that moment I grabbed a can of spray paint I had waiting in the front seat of the car. "You mean, like this?" After shaking the can, I began frantically spraying black enamel on my armored walls of epoxy-treated paint. They watched me in shock and amazement. I began my assault quietly, then exploded with a roar of power that Elijah would have been proud of. "I suppose someone could try to paint over these lovely walls . . . but then it wouldn't stick to the super-treated, God-inspired, Spirit-protected, sin-resistant, Satan-repellent walls of this great and God-fearing church!" My eyes were wild with frenzy.

They stared at me in fear. With a smile I said, "No paint will stick to these walls, boys. Go ahead and give it a try yourself." Then I handed the can of paint to them. No one took it. "Well, boys, gotta go back to work," I told them politely. "Maybe I'll see you around. Huh?" Then I walked into the side door of the church, punched my fist in the air, and said, "Yes!"

Jesus is noted to have burned with frustration a few times. In one particular instance it had to do with something very precious: His Sabbath.

Much more important than the walls of my church were to me, the Sabbath is Christ's connection to people. Shut down the connection—and He gets hot under the collar. Not out of selfishness, but from a heart that beats with a mighty love for His creation, and anything that gets in the way is liable to free His anger. Take a look at the bold way He makes clear the importance of real Sabbathkeeping.

Life of Christ

Mark 3:1-5

"Another time he went into the synagogue, and a man with a shriveled hand was there. Some of them were looking for a reason to accuse Jesus, so they watched him closely to see if he would heal him on the Sabbath. Jesus said to the man with the shriveled hand, 'Stand up in front of everyone.' Then Jesus asked them, 'Which is lawful on the Sabbath: to do good or to do evil, to save life or to kill?' But they remained silent. He looked around at them in anger and, deeply distressed at their stubborn hearts, said to the man, 'Stretch out your hand.' He stretched it out, and his hand was completely restored."

We Believe

The Sabbath

"The beneficent Creator, after the six days of Creation, rested on the seventh day and instituted the Sabbath for all people as a memorial of Creation. The fourth commandment of God's unchangeable law requires the observance of this seventh-day Sabbath as the day of rest, worship, and ministry in harmony with the teaching and practice of Jesus, the Lord of the Sabbath. The Sabbath is a day of delightful communion with God and one another. It is a symbol of our redemption in Christ, a sign of our sanctification, a token of our allegiance, and a foretaste of our eternal future in God's kingdom. The Sabbath is God's perpetual sign of His eternal covenant between Him and His people. Joyful observance of this holy time from evening to evening, sunset to sunset, is a celebration of God's creative and redemptive acts."*

a. Genesis 2:1-3

b. Exodus 20:8-11

c. Deuteronomy 5:12-15

d. Exodus 31:13-17

e. Luke 4:16

f. Ezekiel 20:12, 20

g. Matthew 12:1-12

h. Isaiah 58:13, 14

i. Isaiah 56:5, 6

Which verse speaks to you the most about this topic?

What do you think God would want us to be doing, thinking, and experiencing on the Sabbath? Why?

Way to Pray

As you pray this week, begin by talking to God openly and honestly about your Sabbath experience. Whether it has been meaningful or a struggle, you should discuss with the Lord of the Sabbath the gift He has given you. Make the joy and beauty of the Sabbath hours something you pray about this week so that it might be a blessing to you and to God.

More Than Words

Look up the word "Sabbath" in an exhaustive concordance and focus on the passages in the four Gospels that describe what Jesus did on it. Begin planning with your partner, group, or family to do on the next Sabbath the kind of things Jesus did. You might have to reorganize your day a bit.

Interview someone who you think has a joyful walk with God on the Sabbath. Ask them:
In your own words, share what you think the Sabbath day is all about.
Describe the Sabbath day that has been the most memorable for you. What happened? What did you do? Why is this a good memory for you?
What passage or story from the Bible most demonstrates the importance of the Sabbath to you?

In the Mirror

Think about the attitudes and feelings you have about the Sabbath and write some of your thoughts down about what you hope for in your walk with God—especially on the Sabbath.

* *Seventh-day Adventists Believe*, p. 248.

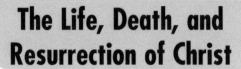

The Life, Death, and Resurrection of Christ

Opening Story

Abandonment. The only question more pressing than "Why?" is "How?" How can a mother and father leave a newborn baby in a dumpster?

"A few hours after giving birth in March in a Fairfax motel room, Abigail Caliboso left her baby, wrapped in a cotton towel, on the floor of a portable toilet at a construction site in Delaware. The 19-year-old nursing student from Woodbridge and the baby's father, Jose Ocampo, 18, of Chantilly, were too frightened to tell their families that they had had a child." [1]

How does this happen? The Washington *Post* article indicated abandonments are often acts of fear because those who do them are typically "good kids." They have good grades, good jobs, and are good athletes—just good people from good families who made a tragic mistake. In desperation they abandon their baby because the shame is too great. Why? How? Here is what some think:

"Some researchers believe that during childbirth a psychotic reaction can occur that is similar to what can happen in other severely stressful situations—for example, soldiers under fire—and that that reaction can compel a woman to try to rid herself of the newborn. Others contend that abandonment or neonaticide is the act of an emotionally immature, self-centered woman who may be distraught over the effect a baby will have on her life." [2]

Jesus on Calvary cried, "My God, My God, why have You forsaken Me?"

Forsaken—the anguish of being abandoned. Was God, like the researchers say, experiencing "a psychotic reaction"? While it may be that those who abandon their children are not in their "right mind," the experience of having your Father abandon you to death on a cross was not a reaction, but God's planned action: "The reason my Father loves me is that I lay down my life—only to take it up again. No one takes it from me, but I lay it down of my own accord. I have authority to lay it down and authority to take it up again. This command I received from my Father" (John 10:17, 18).

Planned, premeditated, intentional abandonment. But God is no criminal here—He's a champion! He did it not out of self-protection or fear, but out of sacrifice and love for lost humanity. What Christ came to do He did with a clear mind.

Life of Christ

Matthew 27:45-51

"From the sixth hour until the ninth hour darkness came over all the land. About the ninth hour Jesus cried out in a loud voice, 'Eloi, Eloi, lama sabachthani?'—which means, 'My God, my God, why have you forsaken me?' When some of those standing there heard this, they said, 'He's calling Elijah.' Immediately one of them ran and got a sponge. He filled it with wine vinegar, put it on a stick, and offered it to Jesus to drink. The rest said, 'Now leave him alone. Let's see if Elijah comes to save him.' And when Jesus had cried out again in a loud voice, he gave up his spirit. At that moment the curtain of the temple was torn in two from top to bottom. The earth shook and the rocks split."

We Believe

The Life, Death, and Resurrection of Christ

"In Christ's life of perfect obedience to God's will, His suffering, death, and resurrection, God provided the only means of atonement for human sin, so that those who by faith accept this atonement may have eternal life, and the whole creation may better understand the infinite and holy love of the Creator. This perfect atonement vindicates the righteousness of God's law and the graciousness of His character; for it both condemns our sin and provides for our forgiveness. The death of Christ is substitutionary and expiatory, reconciling and transforming. The resurrection of Christ proclaims God's triumph over the forces of evil, and for those who accept the atonement assures their final victory over sin and death. It declares the Lordship of Jesus Christ, before whom every knee in heaven and on earth will bow." [3]

a. John 3:16

b. Isaiah 53

c. 1 Peter 2:21, 22

d. 1 John 2:2; 4:10

e. Colossians 2:15

f. Philippians 2:6-11

Which verse above speaks most to you personally about the meaning of the life of Christ?

In your own words, describe the significance of Jesus' life, death, and resurrection?

Way to Pray

Before you pray this week, browse through the four Gospels and scan through the stories. Imagine the stories as they unfold, then talk to God about what you see.

More Than Words

Interview someone who is familiar with the life of Jesus. Ask them:

If you had to choose three stories from the life of Christ to show someone what Jesus' life was about, which ones would you choose and why?

In the Mirror

Think about the final moments of Christ's life and present your thoughts, ideas, feelings, and wonderings in any way you like: pictures, phrases, words to a song, etc.

---

[1] Washington *Post,* Oct. 20, 2000.
[2] *Ibid.*
[3] *Seventh-day Adventists Believe,* p. 106.

The Lord's Supper

Open Questions

When have you had your whole world turned upside down in a matter of seconds? What happened?

Opening Story

"Do you understand what I have done for you?" It is kind of hard to answer that question, isn't it? Especially if you are Peter or any one of the other disciples, because you have seen ordinary moments turn into eternal monuments in just a matter of seconds.

It was just your average bad day at the lake fishing—then *Bam!* Jesus turns it into the most net-ripping, phenomenal fish catch in the history of Galilee.

One minute you're listening to Jesus teach in the Temple when BAM!, you witness the scandal, the showdown, the finger writing in the dirt, the rocks dropping to the ground, and one by one the accusers vanish and grace wins.

"We were just going for a hike up the mountain," one of the disciples remembers, "then all of a sudden the sky splits open, we're blinded by light, we see Moses and

Elijah, and I heard God's voice! What is going on here?"

"He was just doing the Scripture reading in church," another disciple comments, "saying, 'Today this is fulfilled,' and the next thing I see is the whole church trying to toss Him over a cliff."

"One day we pulled over to the side of the road to respectfully let a funeral go by," still another disciple recounts. "I was watching Jesus. He took one look at that grieving mother's face, and all of a sudden He's in the middle of the road with His hand held up like a traffic cop, saying, 'Stop right here!' In just a few seconds the dead boy was talking! Man, I will never forget that moment when Jesus put the boy that had died right in front of the mom like a Mother's Day present just waiting to be opened. I will never, ever forget that day."

It can happen in a moment. If you've been with Jesus, you know that anything can happen in the flicker of a second. The bread and the juice, the water and the washing of the feet. In a moment the disciples saw what history had been waiting for: the sacrifice and the servant. The One who would come and redeem by the shedding of blood and restore all by making everything new with water. And Jesus wanted to know if they were paying attention. He used the Communion service to declare, "This is our flag. When you see it, remember what it stands for." As you look at the life of Christ, notice how important it is to Jesus that we "get it" and how precious this service is to the church when He is gone.

Life of Christ

John 13:1-12

"It was just before the Passover Feast. Jesus knew that the time had come for him to leave this world and go to the Father. Having loved his own who were in the world, he now showed them the full extent of his love. The evening meal was being served, and the devil had already prompted Judas Iscariot, son of Simon, to betray Jesus. Jesus knew that the Father had put all things under his power, and that he had come from God and was returning to God; so he got up from the meal, took off his outer clothing, and wrapped a towel around his waist. After that, he poured water into a basin and began to wash his disciples' feet, drying them with the towel that was wrapped around him. He came to Simon Peter, who said to him, 'Lord, are you going to wash my feet?' Jesus replied, 'You do not realize now what I am doing, but later you will understand.' 'No,' said Peter, 'you shall never wash my feet.' Jesus answered, 'Unless I wash you, you have no part with me.' 'Then, Lord,' Simon Peter replied, 'not just my feet but my hands and my head as well!' Jesus answered, 'A person who has had a bath needs only to wash his feet; his whole body is clean. And you are clean, though not every one of you.' For he knew who was going to betray him, and that was why he said not every one was clean. When he had finished washing their feet, he put on his clothes and returned to his place. 'Do you understand what I have done for you?' he asked them."

We Believe

The Lord's Supper

"The Lord's Supper is a participation in the emblems of the body and blood of Jesus as an expression of faith in Him, our Lord and Saviour. In this experience of Communion Christ is present to meet and strengthen His people. As we partake, we joyfully proclaim the Lord's death until He comes again. Preparation for the Supper includes self-examination, repentance, and confession. The Master ordained the service of foot washing to signify renewed cleansing, to express a willingness to serve one another in Christlike humility, and to unite our hearts in love. The Communion service is open to all believing Christians."*

a. 1 Corinthians 10:16, 17; 11:23-30
b. Matthew 26:17-30
c. Revelation 3:20
d. John 6:48-63
e. John 13:1-17

Which verse speaks to you the most about this topic?

Way to Pray

Write a prayer to God this week that emphasizes what you want to remember as you take Communion. You can start the prayer like this: "Dear God, when I have Communion I want to remember . . ." Be specific, because the more specific our thoughts are, the more we remember.

More Than Words

Find out when the next Communion service is scheduled in your church and plan a week ahead of time (write it in your calendar or whatever you use to keep track of important events) to remind yourself of what you want to remember as you participate. Interview an elder, deacon, or deaconess in the church and ask them to respond to the following questions:

What Communion service was most memorable for you? Why?

Why do you think this service is so important to each individual in the church? Why is it vital to the church as an entire congregation?

What do you think about when you wash the other person's feet? How do you feel when someone is washing yours?

What's going on in your heart and mind when you eat the bread and drink the juice?

In the Mirror

Think about and write down what you have observed about the Communion service already and what you want to experience in the future.

_____

* *Seventh-day Adventists Believe*, p. 194.

Spiritual Gifts

On the continuum below, indicate what you think represents your church family in the area of active participation and responsibility:

1—Almost everyone (90-100 percent of the members) is doing the work of the church.

5—Only a few (10-20 percent of the members) are doing the entire work of the church.

1	2	3	4	5

Almost everyone   **Only a few**

Why do you think this is the case in your church? What would you like to see happen in your church when it comes to getting people involved?

Opening Story

Nothing breeds competition like the game "Capture the Flag." Unfortunately, when I learned to play it I was at the age when the girls had already grown a bit faster than the boys. The girls on my block were stronger, faster, and meaner, and probably more vicious than kickboxers. Needless to say, they beat us every time.

This time would be different, though. Matt had a plan. At least that's why we huddled together in a tight circle of preteen camaraderie. His face was intense. "OK, guys, we have to win this time. I hate losing to those girls. I have a plan!"

The others chimed in, "Yeah, that's what we need. A plan!"

Two years younger than the rest of the boys, I eagerly watched as everyone became silent and attentive. "Here's what we are going to do," he began. Someone popped their head out of the huddle to see if the girls were inching their way closer to hear what our plan was. But they weren't.

"Everyone is going to stand around the field and pretend they are guarding a flag," Matt continued. All eyes focused on him as we waited for the rest of the plan. Matt just stared back at us as if he had just shared a national security secret.

William piped up in a high-pitched voice, "That's your plan? Stand around and pretend we're guarding a flag? You call that a plan?"

Matt was crushed. Then, regaining his composure, he said, "Yes, we have to pretend we know something."

"But we don't," Freddie said, admitting the obvious.

"That's right," Matt replied with a grin. "But while the girls are wondering what we are up to, Troy is going to sneak around the back of the park and get the flag!"

At first mutiny flared up. "Troy can't make it past the girls' guard," one of my brother's friends mentioned painfully.

"Yeah," everyone agreed.

Matt, like a true captain, settled his crew down and said, "The girls won't even notice Troy! They never notice Troy!" (I was a little offended by that.) But then the brilliance of his plan began to sink in like milk into a cookie.

"Yeah," they chanted in a whisper. "They'll be watching us, and when we're not attacking, they'll be thinking about where our flag is instead of watching their own."

We broke from the huddle and concentrated on the plan. Meanwhile, scared to death, I unobtrusively made my way around the trees to the back of the girls' domain. Now behind enemy lines, I had never made it this close before. The flag was only yards away, and just as Matt said, no girls were guarding it. They were in fact huddling together to figure out which boy was guarding the boys' flag. When I looked for Matt, he gave me the nod. My heart felt like bursting through my 10-year-old chest as I leaped out from behind the trees and raced for the flag. The rest was a blur to me. I reached the flag, and still no girls noticed what I was doing. Clutching the white T-shirt (flag) from the top of a picnic table (the girls were so confident they didn't even need to hide it) I raced for the line of safety. At that point the boys darted far into the danger zone to distract the girls from seeing me, but for some reason I began to laugh out loud as I ran. It mixed a bit of scoffing with an element of celebration. Perhaps it was a little too soon to be laughing, but I couldn't help myself. Still, the girls figured out the plan a little too late to catch me. As I crossed the goal line, the boys were waiting for me and piled atop me with shouts of victory. We did a few "in your face" dances in front of the dumbstruck girls because we knew that it would probably be the only time we'd ever get away with the stunt—so we milked it for all it was worth. What a day. At least that's how I remembered it.

"That's your plan?"

"You call that a plan?"

Imagine the scene—a whole countrysideful of people coming to Jesus with diseases, questions, demons, and doubts and fears. As they spread out before Him like a sea of misery, Jesus reveals His plan to fix the whole mess. You want to hear it? Check it out. It doesn't sound like much of a plan, but give it a chance—let it sink in, and you may see Jesus not as a crazy dreamer, but as a wise general whose plan just may work.

Life of Christ

Matthew 9:35–10:1

"Jesus went through all the towns and villages, teaching in their synagogues, preaching the good news of the kingdom and healing every disease and sickness. When he saw the crowds, he had compassion on them, because they were harassed and helpless, like sheep without a shepherd. Then he said to his disciples, 'The harvest is plentiful but the workers are few. Ask the Lord of the harvest, therefore, to send out workers into his harvest field.' He called his twelve disciples to him and gave them authority to drive out evil spirits and to heal every disease and sickness."

What's the plan?

We Believe

Spiritual Gifts

"God bestows upon all members of His church in every age spiritual gifts which each member is to employ in loving ministry for the common good of the church and of humanity. Given by the agency of the Holy Spirit, who apportions to each member as He wills, the gifts provide all abilities and ministries needed by the church to fulfill its divinely ordained functions. According to the Scriptures, these gifts include such ministries as faith, healing, prophecy, proclamation, teaching, administration, reconciliation, compassion, and self-sacrificing service and charity for the help and encouragement of people. Some members are called of God and endowed by the Spirit for functions recognized by the church in pastoral, evangelistic, apostolic, and teaching ministries particularly needed to equip the members for service, to build up the church to spiritual maturity, and to foster unity of the faith and knowledge of God. When members employ these spiritual gifts as faithful stewards of God's varied grace, the church is protected from the destructive influence of false doctrine, grows with a growth that is from God, and is built up in faith and love."*

a. Romans 12:4-8
b. 1 Corinthians 12:9-11, 27, 28
c. Ephesians 4:8, 11-16
d. Acts 6:1-7
e. 1 Timothy 3:1-13
f. 1 Peter 4:10, 11

Which verse speaks to you the most about this topic?

Way to Pray

Warning! The way you pray from here on out is dangerous! If you do this, be forewarned, it could change your life drastically.

As you take the spiritual gifts survey, begin to ask God to create opportunities for you to discover your spiritual gifts. Ask God to confirm what others say about you, what you feel God is asking you to do as a member of His church.

More Than Words

Take the Spiritual Gifts Survey at the back of this book. After you find out where your strengths seem to lie, then pick three people you trust to be honest with you and who know you pretty well (a teacher, pastor, parent, older friend, grandparent, church leader, etc.). Ask them to comment on the results of your survey and to answer the following questions:

Have you seen these qualities or gifts in me? How? When?

Are there other qualities you feel God has gifted me with that I need to consider as well?

How do you think I can best make a difference in the work of the church? Be specific.

You and your partner/group should share with each other the insights you have gained from the survey and the interviews and then commit yourselves to do some activities together to practice and experience work relating to your potential spiritual gift. It is the only way you can be sure this is what God is calling you to do.

Write a letter to your pastor or church board, or go in person to either, and share with them your results and experience and ask for a place to serve in the church.

In the Mirror

Think about and write out how you feel about being a player in God's work. What kind of impact do you want to have in the mission of the Seventh-day Adventist Church?

---

* *Seventh-day Adventists Believe*, p. 206.

The Church

Open Questions

Either/Or

The purpose of the church is to foster the spiritual growth of believers, or to serve the community in Christian love. From your perspective, which would you choose and why?

Does the church need modern agents of change or the faithful pioneers of old? Why did you answer the way you did?

Opening Story

Think of the ways people have used to portray the church: As a body. A family. A hospital. A team. A flock of geese. A company of ants. A hive of bees. A chain. The list goes on with countless analogies that describe what the nature and purpose of the church is about. Here is yet another story that describes the church.

"There is a legend of a village in Southern Europe that boasted of a church called 'The House of Many Lamps.' When it was built in the sixteenth century, the architect provided for no light except for a receptacle at every seat for the placing of a lamp. Each Sunday night, as the people gathered, they would bring their lanterns and slip them into their bracket at their seat. When someone stayed away, the darkness became greater for the whole. It was the regular presence of each person that lit up the church." [1]

The problem with analogies is that they all break down at some point. They give some help, but all symbols are only partial and incomplete. Still, sometimes it is enough. If you were to describe the ideal church, what symbol, story, or analogy would you use?

I don't need to tell you this, but only in a perfect world will you have a perfect church. But I saw a perfect picture of church in the life of Christ the other day. Check it out and see if you can "catch a church in the act" in this glimpse into the life of Christ. Discuss it with your partner and compare what you see to what you believe should be the perfect church.

Life of Christ

Mark 2:1-12

"A few days later, when Jesus again entered Capernaum, the people heard that he had come home. So many gathered that there was no room left, not even outside the door, and he preached the word to them. Some men came, bringing to him a paralytic, carried by four of them. Since they could not get him to Jesus because of the crowd, they made an opening in the roof above Jesus and, after digging through it, lowered the mat the paralyzed man was lying on. When Jesus saw their faith, he said to the paralytic, 'Son, your sins are forgiven.' Now some teachers of the law were sitting there, thinking to themselves, 'Why does this fellow talk like that? He's blaspheming! Who can forgive sins but God alone?' Immediately Jesus knew in his spirit that this was what they were thinking in their hearts, and he said to them, 'Why are you thinking these things? Which is easier: to say to the paralytic, "Your sins are forgiven," or to say, "Get up, take your mat and walk"? But that you may know that the Son of Man has authority on earth to forgive sins. . . .' He said to the paralytic, 'I tell you, get up, take your mat and go home.' He got up, took his mat and walked out in full view of them all. This amazed everyone and they praised God, saying, 'We have never seen anything like this!'"

We Believe

The Church

"The church is the community of believers who confess Jesus Christ as Lord and Saviour. In continuity with the people of God in Old Testament times, we are called out from the world; and we join together for worship, for fellowship, for instruction in the Word, for the celebration of the Lord's Supper, for service to all mankind, and for the worldwide proclamation of the gospel. The church derives its authority from Christ, who is the incarnate Word, and from the Scriptures, which are the written Word. The church is God's family; adopted by Him as children, its members live on the basis of the new covenant. The church is the body of Christ, a community of faith of which Christ Himself is the Head. The church is the bride for whom Christ died that He might sanctify and cleanse her. At His return in triumph, He will present her to Himself a glorious church, the faithful of all the ages, the purchase of His blood, not having spot or wrinkle, but holy and without blemish."[2]

   a. Genesis 12:3
   b. Acts 7:38
   c. Ephesians 4:11-15; 3:8-11
   d. Matthew 28:19, 20
   e. Matthew 16:13-20; 18:17
   f. Ephesians 2:19-22, 1:22, 23; 5:23-27
   g. Colossians 1:17, 18

Which passage really speaks to you the most about a church? Why?

Way to Pray

As you pray this week, invite God to speak to you about what you can do to live as a member of the body of Christ. Share with Him what you hope for and then claim responsibility for your part in fulfilling the mission.

Pray for specific missionaries around the world who may be far away but are still part of the same body of Christ.

More Than Words

Interview: Invite someone who has seen many decades of church life to respond to the following questions:

How do you think the church has changed through the years? How is it still the same?

What would you say is the primary purpose for the Seventh-day Adventist Church as a whole? What do you think we should be devoting ourselves to?

What do you think will need to happen in our churches for us to become successful in our mission?

What specifically would you like to see young people do to "be a light" in this community?

In the Mirror

Think and write about your hopes and fears for your local church. Consider what you might do to be an "agent of change" or a "pioneer of old."

[1] *Nelson's Complete Book of Stories,* p. 127.
[2] *Seventh-day Adventists Believe*, p. 134.

Death and Resurrection

An old adage about skydiving declares that "it's not the fall that kills you as much as it is the ground." Death is something that few people want to experience. Rarely do people volunteer joyfully for the experience, save a few misguided or severely hurting people.

What is death? Is it another step into a different existence? Do we get reincarnated? And is it instant bliss for the do-gooders and flaming terror for the bad people? What trips most people up in a conversation about death is that they are talking about the middle of a conversation instead of the whole.

Janet, an academy student of mine, walked around the corner of the hallway at school and overheard part of a conversation. "I walked into the office and Frank was drinking; can you believe it?" one girl said to another as they stood in front of their lockers. Concerned for Frank, who obviously had a drinking problem and was doomed to life as an alcoholic for sure if we didn't intervene immediately, she hurried to my office.

"How do you know this, Janet?" I said, a little suspicious, after she told me what the girl had said.

"I heard some girls talking about it in the hall. No mistaking it, Pastor Troy, we need to do something," she pleaded.

I called up Frank, but he was not at home. So I went to talk with the principal to see if he knew where Frank was. "Frank should be going into surgery about now," he told me with a smile. "He was supposed to have knee surgery early in the morning, but apparently they postponed it a bit because he forgot about the 'no fluids' rule and drank about a quart of water."

Glad I asked, I thought to myself.

If Janet had heard the beginning of the conversation and the end, she would have discovered more than she could have from just the middle. The same is true as we look at the topic of death. When we talk about death, it is not safe or wise to leave out birth or the resurrection. As you study this glimpse into the mind of Christ, notice that Jesus is mostly interested in discussing the resurrection day. Some questions you may need to ask to help balance your study of this topic include: What is a human being? What does it mean to be alive? What does it mean to be dead? What is the resurrection, and who will be resurrected and for what purpose? Is death the end of us, or will there be an end to death?

Life of Christ

John 6:30-40

"So they asked him, 'What miraculous sign then will you give that we may see it and believe you? What will you do? Our forefathers ate the manna in the desert; as it is written: "He gave them bread from heaven to eat."' Jesus said to them, 'I tell you the truth, it is not Moses who has given you the bread from heaven, but it is my Father who gives you the true bread from heaven. For the bread of God is he who comes down from heaven and gives life to the world.' 'Sir,' they said, 'from now on give us this bread.' Then Jesus declared, 'I am the bread of life. He who comes to me will never go hungry, and he who believes in me will never be thirsty. But as I told you, you have seen me and still you do not believe. All that the Father gives me will come to me, and whoever comes to me I will never drive away. For I have come down from heaven not to do my will but to do the will of him who sent me. And this is the will of him who sent me, that I shall lose none of all that he has given me, but raise them up at the last day. For my Father's will is that everyone who looks to the Son and believes in him shall have eternal life, and I will raise him up at the last day.'"

We Believe

Death and Resurrection

"The wages of sin is death. But God, who alone is immortal, will grant eternal life to His redeemed. Until that day death is an unconscious state for all people. When Christ, who is our life, appears, the resurrected righteous and the living righteous will be glorified and caught up to meet their Lord. The second resurrection, the resurrection of the unrighteous, will take place a thousand years later."*

    a. Romans 6:23
    b. 1 Timothy 6:15, 16
    c. Ecclesiastes 9:5, 6
    d. Psalm 146:3, 4
    e. John 11:11-14
    f. Colossians 3:4
    g. 1 Corinthians 15:51-54
    h. 1 Thessalonians 4:13-17
    i. John 5:28, 29
    j. Revelation 20:1-10

Which verse speaks to you the most about this topic?

If someone were to ask you what you believe about death, how would you respond?

Way to Pray

As you pray, think about the different aspects of life, death, and resurrection you might have questions about. Invite God to give you understanding, comfort, hope, and courage.

Think about asking God for an opportunity to be a source of comfort to someone who may be suffering from the loss of a loved one.

More Than Words

Interview someone you know pretty well in the church who has lost someone close to them. (First, though, make sure they feel comfortable talking about it.) Ask them:

What stories or passages from Scripture first brought you the most comfort? What stories or passages bring you the most comfort today? If someone were to ask you about what happens at death, how would you respond to them, given what you know?

(Be sure to thank them and mention how this helps you personally.)

In the Mirror

Think and write about the resurrection day. What do you believe it will be like?

* *Seventh-day Adventists Believe*, p. 348.

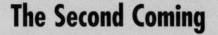

The Second Coming

Open Questions

Agree/Disagree

Most people who are alive at the second coming of Christ will be fully aware of the events and their significance.

Opening Story

"Limited Processing." She looked at me just seething with anger.

"Huh?" I mumbled, a bit shocked by her explosive glare.

"You are a 'limited processor,'" she replied coolly.

I have been called many things in my life, some which I deserve, but most of the time I had at least an idea what the other person meant. Now, though, I was utterly clueless about being a "limited processor" and frankly, a little unsure whether it was good or bad. From my student's attitude I guessed being a "limited processor" was a bad thing. Because I had sought to teach my students that we should be honest with each other, I used the direct approach. "You're mad at me, aren't you?"

"Yes, I am," she erupted. "I was working on the research project you assigned, and that's when I came across this article that says that you're a . . ."

"A limited processor?" I finished.

"Yes" she said, handing me the article. "You made us do a paper on a social issue. I chose the environment crisis. You are constantly doing irresponsible things to the environment. You don't process the issues! That makes you a . . ."

"OK," I said before she could call me that name again. "Show me what you are talking about." She pointed to a portion of an article in *Psychology Today* that focused on the behavior of people on Earth Day. Here is the quote that labeled me a "limited processor."

"Ignorance. Robyn Dawes, Ph.D., a professor at Carnegie Mellon University, blames 'limited processing': People simply don't place their daily behaviors in an environmental context, their decisions are literally thoughtless." [1]

I looked at her, waiting for her to explain further. I was still a little slow with this one. "You use all the lights in the classroom and we need only half of them," she said. "Flip one switch instead of all of them. Like this." She looked as if she were trying to explain something to a child. Then going to the garbage can, she removed my empty plastic water bottle, which I tossed into the trash can at the end of class every day. "And this is abominable. Do you know how long this will take to decompose?" I didn't answer. "Please recycle your plastic bottles! And paper. Why can't we e-mail our assignments and save paper? We have all this paper stuff, and we don't need it." Finally she finished her tirade. It took me awhile, but I finally got it.

Debbie's frustration was real and, for the most part, true. I know the issues that surround the problem of our environment, but I'd never let them sink in deep enough to change the way I lived each day. To a certain degree, we are all "limited processors," and even Jesus would agree with Debbie about her frustration as she watched me day by day in the full knowledge of "the truth" about throwaway bottles, paper, and electricity. Jesus mirrored that frustration because of the resistance to His message. He warned the people of His time about the day of destruction (Jerusalem destroyed in A.D. 70), but they didn't see it. Before He returns, many people will have heard that Christ is coming, many will have seen the signs and known the facts, but the message will have never penetrated. The key for us is to see, hear, and know, but most of all, let it sink in deep enough to change the way we live.

Life of Christ

Luke 19:37-44

"When he came near the place where the road goes down the Mount of Olives, the whole crowd of disciples began joyfully to praise God in loud voices for all the miracles they had seen: 'Blessed is the king who comes in the name of the Lord!' 'Peace in heaven and glory in the highest!' Some of the Pharisees in the crowd said to Jesus, 'Teacher, rebuke your disciples!' 'I tell you,' he replied, 'if they keep quiet, the stones will cry out!' As he approached Jerusalem and saw the city, he wept over it and said, 'If you, even you, had only known on this day what would bring you peace—but now it is hidden from your eyes. The days will come upon you when your enemies will build an embankment against you and encircle you and hem you in on every side. They will dash you to the ground, you and the children within your walls. They will not leave one stone on another, because you did not recognize the time of God's coming to you.'"

How is this story of Jerusalem's destruction descriptive of the scene of the Second Coming?

We Believe

The Second Coming

"The second coming of Christ is the blessed hope of the church, the grand climax of the gospel. The Saviour's coming will be literal, personal, visible, and worldwide. When He returns, the righteous dead will be resurrected, and together with the righteous living will be glorified and taken to heaven, but the unrighteous will die. The almost complete fulfillment of most lines of prophecy, together with the present condition of the world, indicates that Christ's coming is imminent. The time of that event has not been revealed, and we are therefore exhorted to be ready at all times."[2]

    a. Revelation 1:7

    b. Matthew 24:43, 44

    c. 1 Thessalonians 4:13-18

    d. 1 Corinthians 15:51-54

    e. 2 Thessalonians 1:7-10; 2:8

    f. Revelation 14:14-20

    g. Revelation 19:11-21

    h. Matthew 24

    i. 2 Timothy 3:1-5

    j. 1 Thessalonians 5:1-6

Which verse speaks to you the most about this topic?

Way to Pray

Take some time to think about the things you get complacent over. Ask God to give you this week a love for the Second Coming, so you can say with John in Revelation, "Even so, Lord, come!"

More Than Words

Interview someone over the age of 20 with the following questions:

When in your life have you thought that God would come right away?

How do you make the reality that Jesus is coming something you can experience every day?

What is your favorite passage or story from the Bible about the second coming of Christ and why?

In the Mirror

Think and write about the confidence you want to have in the last days.

[1] "Why We Are Destroying the Earth," *Psychology Today,* March-April 2000, p. 49

[2] *Seventh-day Adventists Believe,* p. 332.

The Millennium and the End of Sin

Opening Story

You can see it at the end of blowout basketball games. One team has a 20-point lead, 39 seconds remain to play, and the game continues, but the teams are walking around. The winners are smiling, the losers aren't, and everyone kills time just waiting out the clock.

It's over, but the clock still has to tick away. On the cross Jesus' final words were "It is finished!" That phrase sealed Satan's doom and the end of death. Sin had been conquered, Satan had lost. It was over. You can bounce the ball around all you want, but one reality will not change—Satan is done for and sin and death will never reappear again. It seems hard to imagine such a thing when we see how sin still affects everything. But remember what Paul said:

"When the perishable has been clothed with the imperishable, and the mortal with immortality, then the saying that is written will come true: 'Death has been swallowed up in victory.' 'Where, O death, is your victory? Where, O death, is your sting?'" (1 Corinthians 15:54-55).

"It is finished!" It is the cry of One who has already won. And no matter what Satan tries—even the worst scenarios of destruction you can think of—it still will not change the fact that Jesus has won, the believer will be resurrected, and Satan, sin, and their pet dog, "death," will be no more. It was this notion that fired up the early church. No torture, no persecution, no threat could shake them. Why? Because the game has been won, and now it's all about the countdown of the seconds remaining.

The battle between Christ and Satan is over. But you and I still have to choose which team we want to finish with. It doesn't seem right, I know, but imagine you are watching the NBA finals, and at the last minute you and your friends get to join the winning team. It has a 50-point lead. The choice is a no-brainer—at least you'd think so. Notice the book of Revelation talks about this (underline the phrases and words that help you understand what will happen at the end).

"Blessed and holy are those who have part in the first resurrection. The second death has no power over them, but they will be priests of God and of Christ and will reign with him for a thousand years" (Revelation 20:6).

"He who has an ear, let him hear what the Spirit says to the churches. He who overcomes will not be hurt at all by the second death" (Revelation 2:11).

"But the cowardly, the unbelieving, the vile, the murderers, the sexually immoral, those who practice magic arts, the idolaters and all liars—their place will be in the fiery lake of burning sulfur. This is the second death" (Revelation 21:8).

"Then death and Hades were thrown into the lake of fire. The lake of fire is the second death" (Revelation 20:14).

You can choose to die the second death or to allow Christ to die it for you. He already has, and it worked. How much more do you need to decide which team to join? It's a no-brainer, but why is it that so few seem to see it that way? I know the clock is still ticking, but I'm thinking there's only a few seconds left.

Life of Christ

John 19:25-30

"Near the cross of Jesus stood his mother, his mother's sister, Mary the wife of Clopas, and Mary Magdalene. When Jesus saw his mother there, and the disciple whom he loved standing nearby, he said to his mother, "Dear woman, here is your son,' and to the disciple, 'Here is your mother.' From that time on, this disciple took her into his home. Later, knowing that all was now completed, and so that the Scripture would be fulfilled, Jesus said, 'I am thirsty.' A jar of wine vinegar was there, so they soaked a sponge in it, put the sponge on a stalk of the hyssop plant, and lifted it to Jesus' lips. When he had received the drink, Jesus said, 'It is finished.' With that, he bowed his head and gave up his spirit."

We Believe

The Millennium and the End of Sin

"The millennium is the thousand-year reign of Christ with His saints in heaven between the first and second resurrections. During this time the wicked dead will be judged; the earth will be utterly desolate, without living human inhabitants, but occupied by Satan and his angels. At its close Christ with His saints and the Holy City will descend from heaven to earth. The unrighteous dead will then be resurrected, and with Satan and his angels surround the city; but fire from God will consume them and cleanse the earth. The universe will thus be freed of sin and sinners forever."*

    a. Revelation 20
    b. 1 Corinthians 6:2, 3
    c. Jeremiah 4:23-26
    d. Revelation 21:1-5
    e. Malachi 4:1
    f. Ezekiel 28:18, 19

Which verse speaks to you the most about this topic?

As you understand the events of the end of time and the end of Satan's existence, draw out a little timeline indicating what you think will happen and when.

Way to Pray

Think about the verses you have just studied. God has given you enough information to make you confident about where you stand both now and in the days to come. Pray this week in thankfulness for what God has already done and what He promises to do in the last days.

More Than Words

Interview someone with the following questions:

How do you explain how a God of love could destroy the world by fire? Doesn't that seem harsh to you?

What story or passage from the Bible gives you the most confidence and assurance that your life is safe in God's hands?

In the Mirror

Think and write about God's character as you see it—both His amazing grace and the fact that He will punish the wicked by fire. How does that all fit together for you?

---

* *Seventh-day Adventists Believe*, p. 362.

The New Earth

Joe is a friend of mine. I love him, but he's . . . well . . . cheap. I hate to say it like that, but since his wife, Jenny, came right out with it, I guess I can too. Joe makes enough money to buy his wife a new car, but he won't. Now, I'm not going to share all the conversations we have had about this topic, but needless to say Joe finally broke down, and we went shopping for a new car for his wife.

Although Joe almost had a nervous breakdown haggling with the dealer, we finally purchased the car (I say we because I had to literally force his hand to sign the check). He wanted it to be a surprise, so we parked the car beforehand at a restaurant. They had a wonderful dinner together. Then, as they were beginning to leave, he said, "Jenny, I have a present for you, but I want it to be a surprise, so I'm going to blindfold you."

Jenny rarely received surprises from him, so she didn't want to ruin her chances by asking too many questions. He led her out to the new car, unlocked it with the remote key, and opened the door. A smile crept across her face and blossomed into laughter as she sat down in the brand-new car.

"I can't believe you bought me a brand-new car," she said, not taking the blindfold off.

"How do you know it is a new car, Jenny? You haven't even seen it," Joe said in shock. "You have never had a new car before, so how can you tell?"

"I can tell it's new because it smells new," she cooed.

Joe left it at that. And so should we. I have heard too many questions about what we will eat, what we will do and not do, or whom we will be married to or not married to in heaven. It is all fascinating, but I know only two things for sure:

1. Heaven will be new.

2. I will not argue or be disappointed in whatever the arrangements are.

Take the passages you find in God's Word and let them give you the basic idea and then you can dream on. Many will ask questions and make claims about heaven, but don't miss the point, as did the Pharisees and Sadducees in Christ's day. They weren't interested in heaven—they wanted the head of Jesus. Consider this story as you study about heaven and the new earth.

Life of Christ

Mark 10:17-31

"As Jesus started on his way, a man ran up to him and fell on his knees before him. 'Good teacher,' he asked, 'what must I do to inherit eternal life?' 'Why do you call me good?' Jesus answered. 'No one is good—except God alone. You know the commandments: "Do not murder, do not commit adultery, do not steal, do not give false testimony, do not defraud, honor your father and mother."' 'Teacher,' he declared, 'all these I have kept since I was a boy.' Jesus looked at him and loved him. 'One thing you lack,' he said. 'Go, sell everything you have and give to the poor, and you will have treasure in heaven. Then come, follow me.' At this the man's face fell. He went away sad, because he had great wealth. Jesus looked around and said to his disciples, 'How hard it is for the rich to enter the kingdom of God!' The disciples were amazed at his words. But Jesus said again, 'Children, how hard it is to enter the kingdom of God! It is easier for a camel to go through the eye of a needle than for a rich man to enter the kingdom of God.' The disciples were even more amazed, and said to each other, 'Who then can be saved?' Jesus looked at them and said, 'With man this is impossible, but not with God; all things are possible with God.' Peter said to him, 'We have left everything to follow you!' 'I tell you the truth,' Jesus replied, 'no one who has left home or brothers or sisters or mother or father or children or fields for me and the gospel will fail to receive a hundred times as much in this present age (homes, brothers, sisters, mothers, children and fields—and with them, persecutions) and in the age to come, eternal life. But many who are first will be last, and the last first.'"

We Believe

The New Earth

"On the new earth, in which righteousness dwells, God will provide an eternal home for the redeemed and a perfect environment for everlasting life, love, joy, and learning in His presence. For here God Himself will dwell with His people, and suffering and death will have passed away. The great controversy will be ended, and sin will be no more. All things, animate and inanimate, will declare that God is love; and He shall reign forever. Amen."*

a. 2 Peter 3:13

b. Isaiah 35

c. Isaiah 65:17-25

d. Matthew 5:5

e. Revelation 21:1-7; 22:1-5; 11:15

In your own words, share how you would explain the heaven and the new earth to a child in kindergarten.

Way to Pray

As you pray this week, ask God to keep you focused on living in the mind-set of the new earth.

More Than Words

Interview someone with the following questions:
What are you looking forward to about the new earth the most?
What promise from Scripture best helps you understand what heaven will be like?

In the Mirror

Think and write about what you imagine the earth will be like when Christ makes it new all over again.

---

* *Seventh-day Adventists Believe*, p. 374.

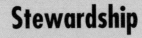

Stewardship

Open Questions

Rank the following in order of importance to you, 1 being the most and 5 being the least.

What God wants most from us?

___ Time

___ Service

___ Money and Resources

___ Talents

___ Mind and Heart

Why?

Rank what you think demonstrates our commitment to God the most:

___ Time

___ Service

___ Money and Resources

___ Talents

___ Mind and Heart

Why?

Opening Story

"Get off of my property!" the girl screamed.

"The sidewalk is not your property; it's government property, so there!" the boy said.

The argument raged on while I raked up the leaves on the lawn next door to the battle. I realized that I used to participate in arguments almost identical to this, but my patience for such belligerence now wore thin. Although I don't want to be known in the neighborhood for being the mean dad, I had had enough. What I did to stifle the arrogant stubbornness of the trespasser may have been somewhat dubious. But while I don't make a practice of it, still it was more than a little fun.

I went inside and called a friend of mine and made arrangements for the boy outside to speak directly to the government about whose property he was standing on. Then returning outside, I continued to rake leaves while the girl screamed, "It's my property! Get off!"

"I can stand here on the sidewalk and do whatever I want because it's government property," the boy replied.

My cell phone rang. After answering the phone, I assumed a convincing expression of concern and mentioned the boy's name with a questioning look on my face. "Billy? Yeah, he's right here." I think it was the first time anyone had ever called him on a cell phone. "Billy, it's for you."

"Me?" he replied in disbelief. I handed him the phone and watched, barely able to keep from bursting into laughter. "Hello," Billy said, puzzled. He was silent as he listened, but looked around as if some unseen watcher were observing him. Then without another word he handed me the phone and walked quickly back to his home, glancing around as though someone were watching him. Every once in a while Billy still paused in the middle of playing to see if he could spot the unseen watcher.

The issue of ownership rights to the sidewalk is still under way in many neighborhoods. But for every believer in Christ, the Lord is sole owner of not only our stuff, but also us. Paul said, "Do you not know that you belong to Christ?"

In our world people struggle to acquire and own things. *Our resources, our own lives, belong to me,* we think. "It's my life!" says the average person today. But the Christian at baptism declares, "It's not my life." You no longer live, but Christ lives within you.

The kind of selfless giving that grows out of an attitude of knowing who owns everything enables us to contribute to God's cause instead of our own interests.

Notice how Jesus emphasizes selflessness in giving.

Life of Christ

Matthew 6:1-4

"Be careful not to do your 'acts of righteousness' before men, to be seen by them. If you do, you will have no reward from your Father in heaven. So when you give to the needy, do not announce it with trumpets, as the hypocrites do in the synagogues and on the streets, to be honored by men. I tell you the truth, they have received their reward in full. But when you give to the needy, do not let your left hand know what your right hand is doing, so that your giving may be in secret. Then your Father, who sees what is done in secret, will reward you."

We Believe

Stewardship

"We are God's stewards, entrusted by Him with time and opportunities, abilities and possessions, and the blessings of the earth and its resources. We are responsible to Him for their proper use. We acknowledge God's ownership by faithful service to Him and our fellowmen, and by returning tithes and giving offerings for the proclamation of His gospel and the support and growth of His church. Stewardship is a privilege given to us by God for nurture in love and the victory over selfishness and covetousness. The steward rejoices in the blessings that come to others as a result of his faithfulness."*

a. Genesis 1:26-28; 2:15
b. 1 Chronicles 29:14
c. Haggai 1:3-11
d. Malachi 3:8-12
e. 1 Corinthians 9:9-14
f. Matthew 23:23
g. 2 Corinthians 8:1-15
h. Romans 15:26, 27

Which verse speaks to you the most about this topic?

How would you teach the concept of stewardship to a fourth grader?

Way to Pray

Write a letter to God that gives Him all of the stuff you tend to desperately hold on to. Pray regularly this week for a sense that God is the owner and you are the trusted manager.

More Than Words

Interview someone who has children who are in college or older. Ask the following questions:

When in your life has God come through miraculously for you as a result of your faithful giving?

Why do you think it is hard for us to think of our "things" or even "time" as belonging to God and not to ourselves?

What words of wisdom do you have for someone my age about giving and working in the church?

In the Mirror

Think and write about your desire to make your giving and your serving a regular part of your walk with God.

---

* *Seventh-day Adventists Believe*, p. 268.

Christian Behavior

Open Questions

Agree/Disagree

Christians should stand out in our world because of their dress, entertainment, and health principles.

Why did you answer the way you did?

Opening Story

I read this story and thought it would be a great start to our study on the Christian lifestyle.

"There is a story about two New York men who had never been out of the city. They decided that they had had it with city living, so they bought a ranch down in Texas in order to live off the land like their ancestors.

"The first thing they decided they needed was a mule. So they went to a neighboring rancher and asked him if he had a mule to sell. The rancher answered, 'No, I'm afraid not.'

"They were disappointed, but as they visited with the rancher for a few moments one of them saw some honeydew melons stacked against the barn and asked, 'What are those?' The rancher, seeing that they were hopeless city slickers, decided to have some fun. 'Oh,' he answered, 'those are mule eggs. You take one of those eggs home and wait for it to hatch, and you'll have a mule.' The city slickers were overjoyed at this, so they bought one of the melons and headed down the bumpy country road toward their ranch. Suddenly they hit an especially treacherous bump, and the honeydew melon bounced out of the back of the pickup truck, hit the road, and burst open. Now, seeing in his rearview mirror what had happened, the driver turned his truck around and drove back to see if he could retrieve his mule egg.

"Meanwhile a big old Texas jackrabbit came hopping by and saw this honeydew melon burst in the road. He hopped over to it, and standing in the middle of that mess he began to eat. Now here came the two city slickers. They spied their mule egg burst open and this long-eared creature in the middle of it. One of the men shouted, 'Our mule egg has hatched! Let's get our mule.'

"But seeing those two men coming toward it, the jackrabbit took off, hopping in every direction with the two city fellows in hot pursuit. The two men from New York gave everything they had to catch him, but finally they could go no farther. Both men fell wearily on the ground gasping for air while the jackrabbit hopped off into the distance. Rising up on his elbow, one of the men said to the other, 'Well, I guess we lost our mule.' The other man nodded grimly. 'Yes, but you know,' he said, 'I'm not sure I wanted to plow that fast anyway.'" [1]

When you make a decision to follow Christ, it is a commitment. Being a Christian today will involve your giving up things that others pursue, doing things others would never think to do, and living a life that stands out as different in our world. Is it worth it? Not if your commitment is only part time or only part of your life or part of your habits or part of your relationships or part of your lifestyle. It just isn't worth it. But full surrender, full commitment, will bring about a life that is full. Count on it.

Life of Christ

Matthew 7:15-29

" 'Watch out for false prophets. They come to you in sheep's clothing, but inwardly they are ferocious wolves. By their fruit you will recognize them. Do people pick grapes from thornbushes, or figs from thistles? Likewise every good tree bears good fruit, but a bad tree bears bad fruit. A good tree cannot bear bad fruit, and a bad tree cannot bear good fruit. Every tree that does not bear good fruit is cut down and thrown into the fire. Thus, by their fruit you will recognize them. Not everyone who says to me, "Lord, Lord," will enter the kingdom of heaven, but only he who does the will of my Father who is in heaven. Many will say to me on that day, "Lord, Lord, did we not prophesy in your name, and in your name drive out demons and perform many miracles?" Then I will tell them plainly, "I never knew you. Away from me, you evildoers!" Therefore everyone who hears these words of mine and puts them into practice is like a wise man who built his house on the rock. The rain came down, the streams rose, and the winds blew and beat against that house; yet it did not fall, because it had its foundation on the rock. But everyone who hears these words of mine and does not put them into practice is like a foolish man who built his house on sand. The rain came down, the streams rose, and the winds blew and beat against that house, and it fell with a great crash.' When Jesus had finished saying these things, the crowds were amazed at his teaching, because he taught as one who had authority, and not as their teachers of the law."

We Believe

Christian Behavior

"We are called to be a godly people who think, feel, and act in harmony with the principles of heaven. For the Spirit to re-create in us the character of our Lord we involve ourselves only in those things which will produce Christlike purity, health, and joy in our lives. This means that our amusement and entertainment should meet the highest standards of Christian taste and beauty. While recognizing cultural differences, our dress is to be simple, modest, and neat, befitting those whose true beauty does not consist of outward adornment but in the imperishable ornament of a gentle and quiet spirit. It also means because our bodies are the temples of the Holy Spirit, we are to care for them intelligently. Along with adequate exercise and rest, we are to adopt the most healthful diet possible and abstain from the unclean foods identified in the Scriptures. Since alcoholic beverages, tobacco, and the irresponsible use of drugs and narcotics are harmful to our bodies, we are to abstain from them as well. Instead, we are to engage in whatever brings our thoughts and bodies into the discipline of Christ, who desires our wholesomeness, joy, and goodness."[2]

a. Romans 12:1, 2

b. 1 John 2:6

c. Ephesians 5:16-26

d. Philippians 4:8

e. 1 Peter 3:1-4

f. 1 Corinthians 6:19, 20

g. Leviticus 11

h. 3 John 2

What do you think these passages are saying about how we should live as followers of Christ?

Which passage speaks to you the most about your lifestyle? Why?

Way to Pray

Make a list of the areas of your life that you want God to guide the most.

As you pray this week, begin each day with a prayer that focuses on a particular part of your personal life and in it ask for His help and guidance in making choices.

More Than Words

What adjustments or commitments do you want to make in order to put your life in harmony with the great plan God has for you? What changes will you make? What will you do that you're not doing now?

Interview a college student or someone older and ask the following questions:

What are the big choices you have had to make about your personal standards as a Christian?

What stories or passages from Scripture are guides for what you choose to eat, wear, listen to, and participate in?

What Bible character would you most like to pattern your life after? Why?

In the Mirror

What things last forever, and what things tend to fade away? Think and write about how you relate to temporary things as opposed to eternal things.

[1] James S. Hewett, *Illustrations Unlimited*, pp. 98, 99.
[2] *Seventh-day Adventists Believe*, p. 278.

Marriage and Family

Open Questions

Rank in order of importance the elements you think are necessary in a successful marriage, 1 being the most important and 5 being the least important of the suggestions listed.

___ Communication
___ Personal and physical attraction
___ Mutual respect
___ United in spiritual goals
___ Common interests and activities

Why?

Opening Story

The retirement home was buzzing with junior high students. They wanted to visit and to sing and to bring some encouragement to the elderly people living in the home. I went to one room where a man named Henry lived. In addition to a number of ailments he was suffering from, he could no longer see.

"I've been blind for so long I don't remember what anything looks like anymore," he told me. (I thought about that for a moment. I can imagine how difficult it would be to have been born blind and not have any way to identify the things that people talk about. But what of those who had seen clearly before they went blind? Can they still remember and visualize in their mind those images? I don't know.) "Do you remember what your favorite scenery looks like?" I asked.

"Nope," he replied quickly. "In my mind I can remember only two things: the sunrise on my daddy's wheat field and Sue Betty Lou Bender's face. She was the most beautiful girl I ever . . ."

My attention drifted as I thought to myself, *Who on earth would name their child . . . ?* Anyway, he remembered two things before his world grew dark—the sunrise and that girl. Two things.

Most humans can't even imagine a world without sin. Sin is so much a part of our world we use the phrase "the world" to describe the totality of what is sinful. However, we still have two things that remind us about the perfect world God created: the Sabbath and marriage. They are precious to God because they are about His relationship to us. The Sabbath reminds us who created us and whom we belong to. And marriage is the experience two people have that can reflect the relationship God wants to have with us. While the marriage relationship is far from what it used to be, it still holds the same place in God's heart as it did in Eden. Notice that the opening of John's Gospel of Jesus begins with a wedding in the second chapter. As you study about God's love for marriage, take a look at "what can be" instead of what is.

Life of Christ

John 2:1-12

"On the third day a wedding took place at Cana in Galilee. Jesus' mother was there, and Jesus and his disciples had also been invited to the wedding. When the wine was gone, Jesus' mother said to him, 'They have no more wine.' 'Dear woman, why do you involve me?' Jesus replied. 'My time has not yet come.' His mother said to the servants, 'Do whatever he tells you.' Nearby stood six stone water jars, the kind used by the Jews for ceremonial washing, each holding from twenty to thirty gallons. Jesus said to the servants, 'Fill the jars with water'; so they filled them to the brim. Then he told them, 'Now draw some out and take it to the master of the banquet.' They did so, and the master of the banquet tasted the water that had been turned into wine. He did not realize where it had come from, though the servants who had drawn the water knew. Then he called the bridegroom aside and said, 'Everyone brings out the choice wine first and then the cheaper wine after the guests have had too much to drink; but you have saved the best till now.' This, the first of his miraculous signs, Jesus performed at Cana in Galilee. He thus revealed his glory, and his disciples put their faith in him. After this he went down to Capernaum with his mother and brothers and his disciples. There they stayed for a few days."

We Believe

Marriage and Family

"Marriage was divinely established in Eden and affirmed by Jesus to be a lifelong union between a man and a woman in loving companionship. For the Christian, a marriage commitment is to God as well as to the spouse, and should be entered into only between partners who share a common faith. Mutual love, honor, respect, and responsibility are the fabric of this relationship, which is to reflect the love, sanctity, closeness, and permanence of the relationship between Christ and His church. Regarding divorce, Jesus taught that the person who divorces a spouse, except for fornication, and marries another, commits adultery. Although some family relationships may fall short of the ideal, marriage partners who fully commit themselves to each other in Christ may achieve loving unity through the guidance of the Spirit and the nurture of the church. God blesses the family and intends that its members shall assist each other toward complete maturity. Parents are to bring up their children to love and obey the Lord. By their example and their words they are to teach them that Christ is a loving disciplinarian, ever tender and caring, who wants them to become members of His body, the family of God. Increasing family closeness is one of the earmarks of the final gospel message."*

 a. Genesis 2:18-25
 b. Matthew 19:3-9
 c. 2 Corinthians 6:14
 d. Ephesians 5:21-33
 e. Matthew 5:31, 32
 f. Exodus 20:12
 g. Ephesians 6:1-4
 h. Proverbs 22:6

Which verse speaks to you the most about this topic?

Way to Pray

Pray this week to God about your present family and ask God to help you become a team player in it.

More Than Words

Interview someone, other than your own parents, who you think honors the marriage relationship: What do you think are the most important skills to have as a spouse? Why do you think they are essential?

What passage or story from Scripture reminds you of your relationship with God and your spouse?

What advice would you give someone my age about marriage (other than "wait until you're a little older")?

In the Mirror

Why do you think God set up the whole system of families? Do you think it was by accident or intentional? What do you think God really wants families to be like?

---

* *Seventh-day Adventists Believe*, p. 294.

Christ's Ministry in the Heavenly Sanctuary

Open Questions

When has someone distracted you from communicating to someone else? What was that like? How did you respond?

Opening Story

My friend teaches art to children. With her ability, she could easily do well in the world of art. However, she chooses to teach art to children—children who are blind. She instructs them in the basic skills of pottery, an art form in which her students can create things and express themselves even though they cannot see.

I stopped by to observe her class one time, but her students were not busy at work. Instead, they were sitting quietly on their stools, apparently waiting for Mrs. Robbins. "Is Mrs. Robbins here?" I asked sheepishly.

"No, she's taking care of the bad guys," a girl said, turning her head my direction. "She'll be back soon."

Bad guys? I thought. *In an art class?* Stepping outside, I could see Mrs. Robbins in the distance speaking to a police officer. "What happened?" I asked afterward.

"Some high school boys have been disrupting my art class by making noise and banging on the windows and running away. They have been at it for a week now, and I finally got them." She punched her fist into the air victoriously.

"What did you do?"

"I just called my friend at the police station, and three cars came down and rounded up the boys and took them back to the high school. I made arrangements for their bikes and skateboards to be impounded as well," she said with a smile.

"Isn't that a bit harsh?" Even as the words fell from my mouth I knew I had made a mistake.

"Do you have any idea how hard it is to teach art to blind children? Not to mention how much more complicated it gets when I have boys outside scaring these children to death?" I didn't think she really wanted me to answer that. "For some of these kids my class is the only opportunity for them to create anything," she continued, "so I'm not going to let a bunch of disrespectful, mindless teenagers get in the way of the best part of their day." Needless to say, I felt my hair singed. Quickly agreeing with her measures, I got away while I could.

After thinking about it, I concluded her response was appropriate. It reminds me of the passion God had for His people:

"Then have them make a sanctuary for me, and I will dwell among them" (Exodus 25:8).

"Then I will dwell among the Israelites and be their God. They will know that I am the Lord their God, who brought them out of Egypt so that I might dwell among them. I am the Lord their God" (Exodus 29:45, 46).

God's passion is to be close to us. He wants us to know Him, especially how He plans to save us. He doesn't want anyone or anything to get in the way! The sanctuary wasn't just an oversized tent for mindless rituals to keep people busy with religious activity. The awe, the blood, the sounds, the smell of incense, the solemn prayers, the light, the sense that God was behind the next door, gave the children of Israel an opportunity to live with God. But don't get in the way when people want to come and be with God! Just like my zealous friend who teaches art, God will not tolerate people distracting others from His great purpose for their lives. Take a look at Jesus in the Temple.

The Temple was *the* place" where people could come to worship, make a sacrifice, and serve God. But some had turned it into a three-ring circus of hucksters, crooks, and political gamers busily haggling that kept people from seeing God. Notice the zeal Jesus had for the place where God and humanity were supposed to meet together.

Life of Christ

John 2:13-22

"When it was almost time for the Jewish Passover, Jesus went up to Jerusalem. In the temple courts he found men selling cattle, sheep and doves, and others sitting at tables exchanging money. So he made a whip out of cords, and drove all from the temple area, both sheep and cattle; he scattered the coins of the money changers and overturned their tables. To those who sold doves he said, 'Get these out of here! How dare you turn my Father's house into a market!' His disciples remembered that it is written: 'Zeal for your house will consume me.' Then the Jews demanded of him, 'What miraculous sign can you show us to prove your authority to do all this?' Jesus answered them, 'Destroy this temple, and I will raise it again in three days.' The Jews replied, 'It has taken forty-six years to build this temple, and you are going to raise it in three days?' But the temple he had spoken of was his body. After he was raised from the dead, his disciples recalled what he had said. Then they believed the Scripture and the words that Jesus had spoken."

The elements of the sanctuary show us Christ's ministry to us, not only at Calvary but today in heaven. Ultimately, the sanctuary was then, and still is, about Jesus.

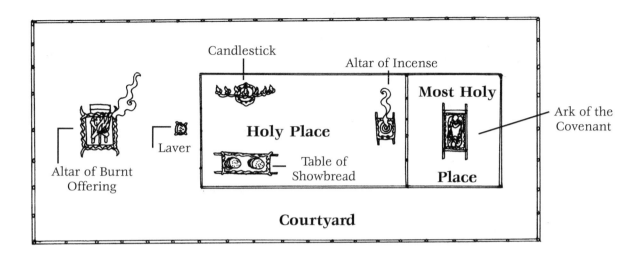

What is the sanctuary?

The courtyard: the altar of burnt offering and the laver. The tent of the sanctuary had two parts: the holy place and the Most Holy Place. The holy place housed the seven-branched candlestick (lampstand), the table of showbread, and the altar of incense.

The Most Holy Place held the ark of the covenant, which contained the Ten Commandments written by God on two tables of stone. Two golden cherubim stood facing each other, and in the middle of the covering was the mercy seat.

What took place at the sanctuary?

As a sinner, you would bring a sacrifice (usually a lamb) and place your hands on the innocent animal. The animal was killed as you confessed your sins, thus in a way placing them on the victim. The priest sprinkled the animal's blood on the altar of burnt offering or in the Holy Place. Every day people transferred their sins to the sanctuary, a practice called the daily sacrifice. Anyone who confessed their sins walked away forgiven.

Because the sanctuary now had the sins of the sinner, it would need to be cleansed once a year. Scripture calls it the Day of Atonement. Essentially, it was a day of judgment in which everyone who had confessed sins throughout the year was judged. It was a moment of awe and solemn reverence. The Levites brought the high priest two goats on the Day of Atonement. The one goat he would sacrifice was called the Lord's goat, while the other was the scapegoat. The high priest sacrificed the Lord's goat and took the blood into the Most Holy Place. The high priest entered this room once a year on this special day and sprinkled the blood on the mercy seat. Then he returned to the holy place and spattered blood on the altar of incense. Next he moved into the courtyard, where he spattered the blood on the altar of burnt offering.

Afterward, the high priest placed his hands on the head of the other goat (the scapegoat) and confessed the sins for a whole year of all the people of Israel and symbolically placed them on the scapegoat. The Levites then sent the scapegoat into the wilderness to wander around until it died with the sins of Israel.

What does it mean?

God showed Moses the sanctuary in heaven, and the one that Moses then built was a model of the one in heaven. The parts of the sanctuary have tremendous meaning and purpose. The sanctuary service demonstrates the two parts of the ministry of Christ (the work of intercession and the work of judgment).

The First Part (the Courtyard and the Holy Place)

When people confessed their sin over the lamb and it was killed and placed on the altar, the act portrayed the sacrifice of Christ as He died on Calvary. (Remember, John the Baptist said, "Behold the Lamb of God who takes away the sins of the world.")

The laver, filled with water, illustrates baptism and the forgiveness of sins as the water washes away the old person of sin.

In the holy place, the table of showbread demonstrates Christ, who is the Bread of life (John 6:35). The candlestick symbolizes that Jesus was the light of the world (John 8:12). The altar of incense depicts the way Christ intercedes for sinners (John 17).

The Second Part (the Most Holy Place)

The ministry of the second compartment involves judgment. The truth about sin is that even though there is forgiveness for sin, someone has to pay. The ark of the covenant is a timeless symbol of God's unchanging law of righteousness. It is important to remember that what makes the sacrifice and the blood and death necessary is God's law. Sin (transgression of the law) brings death. The ark represents God's throne, where His justice calls for an answer to the sin problem.

The scapegoat stands for Satan, who is banished from the sanctuary with the sins of the people. Justice is served, because sin, death, and shame die with the one who is ultimately responsible for them.

The sanctuary is not a sick ritual ordered by an angry God who wants blood. No, quite the opposite, it is a moment to participate in and witness a loving and just God who deals with the sin problem by becoming the payment for sin Himself. Scripture has many wonderful stories of God's love that are warm and fuzzy. But the sanctuary service is not warm and fuzzy—it is God's love conquering the cold, cruel effects of sin. While it is not pretty, it does save.

As you read the passages that describe the heavenly sanctuary and God's plan of salvation also read chapters 23 and 24 in *The Great Controversy* for a more thorough explanation on the work of the sanctuary and Christ's ministry in the sanctuary.

We Believe

Christ's Ministry in the Heavenly Sanctuary

"There is a sanctuary in heaven, the true tabernacle which the Lord set up and not man. In it Christ ministers on our behalf, making available to believers the benefits of His atoning sacrifice offered once for all on the cross. He was inaugurated as our great High Priest and began His intercessory ministry at the time of His ascension. In 1844, at the end of the prophetic period of 2300 days,

He entered the second and last phase of His atoning ministry. It is a work of investigative judgment, which is part of the ultimate disposition of all sin, typified by the cleansing of the ancient Hebrew sanctuary on the Day of Atonement. In that typical service the sanctuary was cleansed with the blood of animal sacrifices, but the heavenly things are purified with the perfect sacrifice of the blood of Jesus. The investigative judgment reveals to heavenly intelligences who among the dead are asleep in Christ and therefore, in Him, are deemed worthy to have part in the first resurrection. It also makes manifest who among the living are abiding in Christ, keeping the commandments of God and the faith of Jesus, and in Him, therefore, are ready for translation into His everlasting kingdom. This judgment vindicates the justice of God in saving those who believe in Jesus. It declares that those who have remained loyal to God shall receive the kingdom. The completion of this ministry of Christ will mark the close of human probation before the Second Advent."*

    a. Hebrews 8:1-5; 4:14-16

    b. Daniel 7:9-27; 8:13, 14; 9:24-27

    c. Numbers 14:34

    d. Ezekiel 4:6

    e. Leviticus 16

    f. Revelation 14:6, 7; 20:12; 14:12; 22:12

Which verse speaks to you the most about this topic?

What did you learn about the plan of salvation that you may not have heard or understood before?

Way to Pray

As you pray, picture Jesus—your High Priest—praying for you and taking your prayers to the Father as a perfect mediator. Think about what He is doing for you now—judging you by His goodness—and then pray with the joy and confidence of His finished work for you.

More Than Words

Interview a pastor, teacher, elder, or someone who you think has a pretty good knowledge of the meaning and purpose of the sanctuary. Ask the following questions:

What do you think is the most significant feature of the sanctuary service?

What story or passage from Scripture reminds you most of God's great work of salvation?

What do you think the sanctuary in heaven is all about?

In the Mirror

As you reflect on this study, what part of the study do you think was the most meaningful part?

---

* *Seventh-day Adventists Believe*, p. 312.

The Remnant and the Mission of the Church

The end of the book of Revelation contains a challenge to faithfulness. The people of God at the end of time will have several marks that distinguish them from others. Those marks, according to the Bible, will be clear. Notice the emphasis Revelation puts on the faithful:

"This calls for patient endurance on the part of the saints who obey God's commandments and remain faithful to Jesus" (Revelation 14:12).

"Do not be afraid of what you are about to suffer. I tell you, the devil will put some of you in prison to test you, and you will suffer persecution for ten days. Be faithful, even to the point of death, and I will give you the crown of life" (Revelation 2:10).

"They will make war against the Lamb, but the Lamb will overcome them because he is Lord of lords and King of kings—and with him will be his called, chosen and faithful followers" (Revelation 17:14).

It is clear that at the end of time God's people will have certain attributes:

1. They keep God's commandments.

2. They will be persecuted for their faith.

3. Their faith will be a deep, abiding love for Jesus and His Word.

The following illustration reminds me of God's remnant people at the end:

"When Pompei was destroyed by the eruption of Mount Vesuvius, there were many people buried in the ruins. Some were found in cellars, as if they had gone there for security. Some were found in the upper rooms of buildings. But where was the Roman sentinel found? Standing at the city gate where he had been placed by the captain, with his hands still grasping his weapon. There, while the earth shook beneath him—there, while the floods of ashes and cinders covered him—he had stood his post. And there, after a thousand years, was this faithful man still to be found."[1]

Jesus spoke to the disciples about being a true follower. As you read the statement below, notice the struggle between the faithful followers and those who are mistaken. Make your choice today about being part of God's faithful followers.

Life of Christ

John 8:30-37

"Even as he spoke, many put their faith in him. To the Jews who had believed him, Jesus said, 'If you hold to my teaching, you are really my disciples. Then you will know the truth, and the truth will set you free.' They answered him, 'We are Abraham's descendants and have never been slaves of anyone. How can you say that we shall be set free?' Jesus replied, 'I tell you the truth, everyone who sins is a slave to sin. Now a slave has no permanent place in the family, but a son belongs to it forever. So if the Son sets you free, you will be free indeed. I know you are Abraham's descendants. Yet you are ready to kill me, because you have no room for my word.'"

We Believe

The Remnant and the Mission of the Church

"The universal church is composed of all who truly believe in Christ, but in the last days, a time of widespread apostasy, a remnant has been called out to keep the commandments of God and the faith of Jesus. This remnant announces the arrival of the judgment hour, proclaims salvation through Christ, and heralds the approach of His second advent. This proclamation is symbolized by the three angels of Revelation 14; it coincides with the work of judgment in heaven and results in a work of repentance and reform on earth. Every believer is called to have a personal part in this worldwide witness."[2]

    a. Revelation 12:17; 14:6-12; 18:1-4

    b. 2 Corinthians 5:10

    c. Jude 3, 14

    d. 1 Peter 1:16-19

    e. 1 Peter 3:10-14

    f. Revelation 21:1-14

Way to Pray

As you pray to God this week, make a list of seven areas of your spiritual life that you want to become more faithful in, and then pray about each one each day this week.

More Than Words

Choose a person in your church who you believe is a faithful follower of Christ and ask the following questions:

From your understanding of the Bible, describe what you think the remnant in the last days is like. Think of a person you believe can be characterized as a faithful follower of Christ. What are some of their qualities and commitments?

In the Mirror

Think about the final moments of earth's history, as you imagine they will be like, and write your hopes and expectations as the old world passes away and the new enters in.

[1] Michael Green, *1500 Illustrations for Biblical Preaching*, p. 143.
[2] *Seventh-day Adventists Believe*, p. 152.

"What's in the Box?"

Spiritual Gifts Survey

Spiritual Gifts Questionnaire for Youth

Instructions for the "What's in the Box?" survey:

"What's in the Box?" is a simple approach to finding and practicing our spiritual gifts. The task for the loving and mission-minded church is to ask, "What's in the Box?" In other words, "What is in our kids that can significantly shape and move our church forward—today?"

Filling out the survey:

1. Indicate whether each statement is:

Almost Never	Rarely	Sometimes	Frequently	Almost Always
1	2	3	4	5

For example, a statement might declare "I get really frustrated when I hear people talking about doing something but not doing it."

If you "almost never" feel that way, then you would circle the 1 under "almost never." If you find that you frequently get upset about that, then you would circle number 4.

2. As you answer all the statements, put the number you chose for each question in the light gray area of the column to the right. You should have 10 numbers in each

column. Add up the total for each column and write the score in the box at the bottom of the chart.

3. The higher scores are in the areas of the gift you might have. The way to know for sure is to practice using those gifts, and as you have success, you will become more certain about the way God has gifted you.

"We have different gifts, according to the grace given us. If a man's gift is prophesying, let him use it in proportion to his faith. If it is serving, let him serve; if it is teaching, let him teach; if it is encouraging, let him encourage; if it is contributing to the needs of others, let him give generously; if it is leadership, let him govern diligently; if it is showing mercy, let him do it cheerfully" (Romans 12:6-8).

The **ChristWise** approach to spiritual gifts is based on Romans 12:6-8. Some studies on spiritual gifts have up to 24 different spiritual gifts as part of their inventory. For young people, we use the passage in Romans because it simplifies the gifts into seven major categories, which are easier for kids to manage.

The following is a summary of the gifts with a short explanation and an example of what that might look like in a young person.

Prophesy

Speaking the wisdom of God

The term *prophesy* might scare people because it carries all kinds of ideas from calling fire down out of heaven to being able to see into the future. While those experiences may occur, the gift of prophecy has more to do with a person's ability to understand and speak wisely on behalf of God. Individuals who have this gift have the ability to be "in tune" with God in a special way. They tend to be willing to speak up, speak out, and go against the flow of peer pressure. You might see it in the way a young person tries to get people to "do the right thing." We don't want to avoid the possibility that they might see "dreams and visions," but mostly the gift involves courage and character and being really perceptive.

Server

Those who just want to get things done have tremendous value to the church. When God lives in such individuals, great things happen for Him. While some may just want to make plans, helpers make lists of the things to do and get started. They feel best when they are working, and even if the details seem menial, they see how the little parts can fit into the big picture. You can see it in children who always have to be helping, constantly volunteering, and can't sit still for very long.

Teacher/Learner

We combine the gift of teacher/learner because most good teachers love learning. Rarely are teachers effective if they are not teachable themselves. In the church, they like to study and discover truth and also enjoy finding the best ways to communicate it. Such kids not only love it when they understand but they enjoy the way they discovered it and seem to be willing to help others learn.

Builder

Builders have the ability to challenge and strengthen others with their words and deeds. Often called the gift of encouragement, it comes from the idea of building a house. We construct a house step by step, piece by piece. It is obvious as well that while it takes time to build a house, it requires only one stick of dynamite or one earthquake or tornado to utterly destroy it. The same is true with our words and actions. Negative words and actions can destroy quickly, but positive affirmation builds gradually. The builder has a special ability to say the right thing at the right time. Desiring to move people forward with their words and actions, they tend to be positive, proactive people.

Giver

Those who joyfully spend their time, talents, service, and resources for good works we call givers. They don't have to have a lot of money to have this gift—most young people don't. But their sacrificial spirit and generosity tend to stick out. What drives them is not the appearance of being a generous person, but that they just feel so good about helping other people that they are free with their time, their stuff, and their energy.

Leader

People have many different ideas about what really makes someone a leader. The word literally means "to stand before," or "to preside." Some think it is the person who is the loudest. One of the best definitions for leadership is "the ability to influence others." This could go both ways (positive or negative). Have you heard some of the stories great leaders tell about their childhood—all the trouble that they caused? Somehow, though, they were able to influence others. The best leaders are ones who tend to get others involved instead of being the one who does everything themselves. A leader who has to do everything is usually a server in the wrong job.

Compassion

The gift of compassion is the natural inclination to show mercy and to bring help and healing to another person. If someone is lonely, hungry, or hurting, the gift of compassion moves people deep within. Such individuals have to do something about a problem. You can see it in those who react to injustice or unfairness. When there is an opportunity to make a difference, they become a part of the healing. The difference between someone with the gift of compassion and someone who is a server is that compassion sees someone in pain sooner than others.

Questions	Answers					Gifts							
	Almost Never	Rarely	Sometimes	Frequently	Almost Always								
I'm very sensitive to what is good and what is not.	1	2	3	4	5								
I am the first person to jump in and help others.	1	2	3	4	5								
I like to be in charge of people.	1	2	3	4	5								
I can sense when others are hurting ,and I reach out to them.	1	2	3	4	5								
I feel that it is my job to provide and continue to give resources to those less fortunate than myself.	1	2	3	4	5								
I want people to work together.	1	2	3	4	5								
I do not like games in which people can lose.	1	2	3	4	5								
I see the Bible as the truth.	1	2	3	4	5								
I want to be appreciated for the tasks I do for others.	1	2	3	4	5								
I have a vision for the future.	1	2	3	4	5								
I don't like to focus on the bad in others.	1	2	3	4	5								
I trust that God will take care of me.	1	2	3	4	5								
I get many tasks done in time.	1	2	3	4	5								
Major decisions are hard for me to make.	1	2	3	4	5								

Questions	Answers					Gifts						
	Almost Never	Rarely	Sometimes	Frequently	Almost Always							
I feel that God directly speaks to me.	1	2	3	4	5							
It is easier for me to do things for others than just to listen and talk to them.	1	2	3	4	5							
I like new goals and new pursuits.	1	2	3	4	5							
I want others to be happy.	1	2	3	4	5							
I don't like others to know how much I give of my re-sources.	1	2	3	4	5							
I have a real sense of respect for those older than I am.	1	2	3	4	5							
I feel best when everyone else is happy.	1	2	3	4	5							
I want to tell others of what God has said to me.	1	2	3	4	5							
I see the needs of others and act on that.	1	2	3	4	5							
I respect those who are older than I and those who have more wisdom than I do.	1	2	3	4	5							
I don't like to hurt others by my actions or words.	1	2	3	4	5							
If I cannot give money or objects, I will give of my time.	1	2	3	4	5							
I get along well with people regardless of their age.	1	2	3	4	5							

Questions	Answers					Gifts
	Almost Never	**Rarely**	**Sometimes**	**Frequently**	**Almost Always**	
When others are hurting I have a hard time thinking about anything else.	1	2	3	4	5	
I can be harsh and blunt when I talk to people.	1	2	3	4	5	
I cannot leave a project until it is completed in the best possible way.	1	2	3	4	5	
I want to work with a good group of people to accomplish a task.	1	2	3	4	5	
I hurt when I see others in pain and sorrow.	1	2	3	4	5	
I love to give of myself and my resources.	1	2	3	4	5	
I feel as if I'm most helpful when I'm in charge.	1	2	3	4	5	
I tend to believe what other people tell me.	1	2	3	4	5	
Sometimes I have a low self-esteem.	1	2	3	4	5	
I prefer to be a follower.	1	2	3	4	5	
I do not let others know when criticism has hurt me.	1	2	3	4	5	
I don't want to be the center of attention.	1	2	3	4	5	
I always give 10 percent of my earnings and then offerings on top of that.	1	2	3	4	5	

Questions	Answers					Gifts
	Almost Never	Rarely	Sometimes	Frequently	Almost Always	
If people don't like me or what I have done, I don't let it upset me.	1	2	3	4	5	
I feel that I can help others by praying.	1	2	3	4	5	
I do not like to be wrong in the opinions I hold.	1	2	3	4	5	
It is easier for me to do a job than find someone to do it.	1	2	3	4	5	
I am good at networking and finding people to help the cause.	1	2	3	4	5	
I enjoy reaching out to those who are sick, or to those who seem upset.	1	2	3	4	5	
I like to cheer people up by what I donate to others.	1	2	3	4	5	
I do not really like to do detailed work.	1	2	3	4	5	
I can't stand it when people fight or are hateful to each other.	1	2	3	4	5	
I want to see others grow deeper in their relationship with Christ.	1	2	3	4	5	
Sometimes I help so much that I don't focus on the spiritual needs of others.	1	2	3	4	5	

Questions	Answers					Gifts						
	Almost Never	Rarely	Sometimes	Frequently	Almost Always							
I like my life to be organized.	1	2	3	4	5							
I don't want people to feel left out or alone.	1	2	3	4	5							
My biggest desire is to share with others what Jesus did for them on the cross.	1	2	3	4	5							
Letting others know how I feel comes pretty easy for me.	1	2	3	4	5							
I notice quickly when others feel left out.	1	2	3	4	5							
I know when others speak if their words are from God.	1	2	3	4	5							
I enjoy being hospitable to others.	1	2	3	4	5							
I tend to be a workaholic.	1	2	3	4	5							
I would enjoy going to a poverty-stricken society to reach out to others.	1	2	3	4	5							
I am happy to do without things so that others can live a better life.	1	2	3	4	5							
I like to dream of better ways to get things done.	1	2	3	4	5							
I tend to think of the other person's feelings.	1	2	3	4	5							
I want to be instrumental in sharing the gospel and changing people's lives.	1	2	3	4	5							

Questions	Answers					Gifts							
	Almost Never	Rarely	Sometimes	Frequently	Almost Always								
I am the first to offer my help in a task that needs to be accomplished.	1	2	3	4	5								
I put my heart and soul into the job and organization that I am a part of.	1	2	3	4	5								
I communicate with people on a one-on-one level, not in large groups.	1	2	3	4	5								
I manage money well.	1	2	3	4	5								
I feel as if I have to win when playing a game.	1	2	3	4	5								
I can sense when people are lying to me.	1	2	3	4	5								
TOTALS													
						P	S	T	B	G	L	C	

P = Prophesy　**T = Teacher**　**G = Giver**　**C = Compassion**

S = Server　**B = Builder**　**L = Leader**